# Regenerating town centres

# Regenerating town centres

Richard Evans

Manchester University Press
Manchester and New York
distributed exclusively in the USA by St. Martin's Press

*Published by* Manchester University Press
Oxford Road, Manchester M13 9NR, UK
and Room 400, 175 Fifth Avenue, New York, NY 10010, USA

*Distributed exclusively in the USA*
*by* St. Martin's Press Inc., 175 Fifth Avenue, New York,
NY 10010, USA

*British Library Cataloguing-in-Publication Data*
A catalogue record for this book is available from the British Library

*Library of Congress Cataloging-in-Publicatiuon Data applied for*

ISBN 0-7190-4718-8 hardback

First published 1997

00 99 98 97 10 9 8 7 6 5 4 3 2 1

Printed in Great Britain
by Bookcraft (Bath) Ltd, Midsomer Norton

# Contents

# List of tables

# Preface

This book grew out of a project entitled 'Liveable Towns and Cities' commissioned by the Civic Trust and conducted by the author, Jon Dawson and Michael Parkinson. I would like to record my gratitude to my colleagues at the Institute and the many people who assisted us with that assignment. Since then, Michael Parkinson has proved an invaluable source of advice and guidance and I am also greatly indebted to close family and friends for offering stylistic comments and proofreading the typescripts.

Events have undoubtedly moved on a great deal since this book was completed in June 1995. Government planning guidance has been further refined, broadly in favour of town centres. Out-of-town cinema and leisure complexes deserve further consideration. Smaller town centres are witnessing equally dramatic transformations as supermarkets extend their dominance. However, policymakers continue to wrestle with the issues raised in the book and I trust it will enable a wider readership to gain additional insight into a subject of increasing topicality.

Richard Evans
Liverpool, October, 1996

# Introduction

There is growing public concern about the state of our town centres. Traditionally, town centres have been the heart, even the apotheosis, of our urban civilisation, where a multitude of commercial, retail, cultural and governmental activities and functions are uniquely concentrated. Recently however, a series of powerful economic, demographic, social and cultural trends have cast doubt upon their pivotal role. Pollution and congestion, competition from out-of-town shopping centres, unsafe streets, the closure of long established shops in our High Streets and their replacement by cheap discount stores have resulted in a loss of identity and appeal. Many wonder whether town centres face terminal decline. To counter this, a new breed of professional town centre manager has appeared on the scene in an attempt to resurrect their fortunes. The pace of change in retailing has been phenomenal. In Warrington central bus station, there is a bus service to whisk shoppers to Ikea, not some latter-day addition to the new town but the Swedish furniture superstore on the outskirts. And one of the country's principal regional 'attractions' in the North East is the Metro regional shopping centre, whilst the town centre of nearby Sunderland looks run down and a shadow of its former self. Talk is now of mass tele-shopping from home. Retailers are rushing to sell goods and services using electronic home shopping services and the Internet. Barclays have even launched a 'virtual shopping mall' which shoppers can 'visit' using a computer and a modem link and where they can make purchases using a credit card. What does all this mean for the traditional High Street?

Although town centres are of considerable topical interest, there is a lack of contemporary, comprehensive analysis on the subject. With exceptions (e.g. Department of Environment (DoE), 1994), many books concentrate on particular issues like retailing, offices, transportation, arts and cultural activities. Few look at the overall dynamics of change such as institutional behaviour, the relations between key interests and the impact of public policy. Many also fail to distinguish different types of town centre and the different views and consumption patterns of users. Finally, few have raised the question whether the condition of town centres reveals anything at all about the state of society and individual and collective values. Should we welcome cheaper provision of town centre services in other locations despite broader concerns about the preservation of more traditional shared spaces which enhance more communal patterns of life? Should we see ourselves only as consumers of different town centre services, minding our own business? Or do we have any collective responsibilities in relation to what is going on around us?

This book reviews recent events in town centres and raises some basic questions:

- What have been the main components of physical change?
- What have been the principal underlying dynamics?
- What have been the main effects of such trends upon the attractiveness of town centres?
- What has been the relative significance of economic restructuring, institutional factors and public policy?
- Will these factors interact in different ways in future?
- Will town centres prove to be an anachronism or do they still possess intrinsic merit as Britain moves towards the beginning of the twenty-first century?
- If town centres are still needed, are current public policies sufficient to protect their status and ensure their viable future or will they need to be amended and developed?

The introductory chapter describes the genesis and evolution of British town centres. Chapters 2–6 examine the main components of physical change focusing upon retailing, transport, offices and the public realm. Chapter 7 investigates the relative influence of key stakeholders in town centres and the way they relate to each other. Chapter 8 assesses the significance and impact of broad shifts in public policy-making over the last thirty years. The final chapter is more prescriptive. It sets out a series of principles for making town centres more appealing. It also counsels that further reform will be necessary if they are to have a viable future.

## References

Department of Environment (1994) ‘Vital and viable town centres: meeting the challenge’, URBED *et al.*, HMSO, London.

# Chapter 1
# Defining town centres

## Introduction

What are the defining characteristics of town centres and how did they come about? What processes have shaped their evolution? In what sense is their present role and rationale different from what it was originally? Are they anachronisms? This scene-setting chapter tackles some basic definitional questions in order to provide a set of compass directions for the remainder of the book. The opening section contrasts different commentators' understanding of town centres. The next section charts their evolution, and the way in which their physical character has changed over time. The third section describes the current role and characteristics of town centres, while the final section portrays their diversity. The conclusion returns to the problem of defining their essence.

## Different ways of seeing town centres

Different perspectives upon the nature of town centres are a reflection of the concerns and motives of particular academic and professional disciplines. Practitioners have adopted physical and mechanistic modes of explanation to explore relationships between land use and transportation systems and distinguish the status of different centres and their constituent functions. Theorists on the other hand have focused more on underlying processes and the institutional power relations shaping the built environment in central locations. Four distinctive views of town centres are summarised here. Each places a different emphasis upon their physical, economic, cultural, psychological and institutional make-up.

*Analysis of physical composition*

The most straightforward approach to defining town centres has focused upon their mix of land uses, morphological character and nodality. Geographers and town planners, in particular, have traditionally sought to define town centres as discrete areas containing higher-order commercial and retail functions which congregate to exploit their accessibility and other agglomeration advantages. Property values, retail turnover, pedestrian flows, spatial concentration of floorspace, size of urban area, have all been used to define the central business district (CBD) and to establish the relative commercial importance of town centres. Some of these measures have proved to be useful mapping tools. They have revealed differing forms of internal specialisation and linkage such as proximity of shops selling the same comparison goods, grouping of entertainment uses, and clustering of financial, legal and related business support services because of the imperatives of personal contact, a prestigious address and convenience to clients. Similarly, analysis of pedestrian activity and other transport flows have highlighted problems associated with uneven demand for infrastructure and the importance of efficient space usage. However, such methods are now widely recognised as narrow, excessively physical and lacking in theoretical justification and explanatory power. The remaining conceptions give much closer attention to underlying processes. Each is here presented briefly. Their relative merits are addressed later in the chapter.

*Economic theory*

Theories of urban land economics offer a more convincing and logical explanation of the distribution of retail and service activities both within and between town centres. The best known are central place theory (Christaller, 1966) and the concept of bid rent (Alonso, 1964). Christaller maintained that towns initially owed their existence to their centrality, in other words their ability to serve surrounding rural areas by providing a range of goods and services. The nature and extent of such services was, in his view, determined by two factors: the minimum size of population necessary for viability and the maximum distance customers are prepared to travel to make a purchase. Later, the relative concentration of different types of goods and services in different centres was used to construct hierarchies of retail centre and also urban rankings. Access times, frequency of purchase and other aspects of purchasing power and consumer behaviour were other important factors.

Bid rent theories are based on the premise that the disposition of land uses is determined primarily by the user's ability to pay rent. Some users place more importance than others upon centrality and accessibility because of their differing locational requirements. Retailers and office users therefore bid up for land in the most central locations and displace other activities such as manufacturing and housing for whom agglomeration advantages are less significant. In addition, the latter are unable to use the land as intensively and have lower margins. Marxists regard the economic utility of land expressed in terms of land values and rents as the key to understanding the development of town centres. The 'rent gap' between the current use value of a site or building and its potential investment value is often taken as a starting point for understanding redevelopment pressures and patterns.

*Centres of public social life*

Many commentators have placed greater emphasis upon the cultural significance of town centres although some of their arguments do relate to the more materialist conceptions. Three schools of thought have emerged. Behavioural psychologists view town centres as places of collective consciousness since some of their principal features, such as squares and monuments, engender a sense of belonging amongst local inhabitants and therefore become symbols of civic identity. Prominent landmarks may also be an important means of personal orientation and self-definition (Lynch, 1960). Demolition of such features often arouses strong feelings and an acute and enduring sense of personal and collective loss.

Others take the view that town centres are a key part of the public domain because they contain a concentration of public cultural assets such as libraries, museums, art galleries, public buildings and open spaces which are also the scene of festivals and street events (Bianchini, 1990). Besides being valuable in their own terms, they are significant because they promote social interaction, raise personal awareness of civic society and offer universal access, irrespective of personal circumstances.

A sharply contrasting view is that town centres are essentially arenas of consumption of retail goods and places of leisure and entertainment. The environment is perceived as the outcome of the interplay between retailer and consumer and social as well as economic factors. Both have a mutual interest in convenience and comfort since this maximises turnover and shopping time. This explains the advent of the enclosed shopping precinct, improvements in circulation arrangements and enhanced customer support services. In other respects, a compromise is struck between factors such as novelty and tradition, standards of presentation and value for money, depending upon the economic conditions, the retail goods in question, and customer profiles and preferences. It is open to dispute to what extent commodification in the form of product packaging and advertising is manipulative, exploitative, dehumanising and destructive of other non-commercial activities, or a reflection of consumer preferences and of wider cultural significance. The 'arts and cultural industries' are particularly ambivalent in this respect.

*Institutional analysis*

Political scientists focus on institutional behaviour and distribution of power and influence which dramatically modify many of the factors described. They view the physical evolution of town centres as reflecting the nature of inter-organisational relations between the main agents of change such as property owners, investors, developers, interest groups and governmental organisations, especially local authority politicians and planning and estate professionals. Concentration of economic power within fewer hands has generated recent interest in the relationship between externally-based elites and local civic interests. The consensus is that local dependence upon external property interests and the flow of international capital into and out of property has grown markedly as a consequence of declining local ownership of business and property and diminished local authority financial resources and influence. None the less, the multiplicity of owners and property rights, coupled with planning regulations, can still fundamentally shape the built environment.

Although these perspectives portray the complexity and multi-faceted nature of town centres, they are not mutually exclusive. Public and private institutions increasingly have to adopt commercial principles, including those with wider cultural and social goals and aspirations. Conversely, many businesses such as cafes, restaurants, pubs and other meeting places potentially fulfil a valuable social function, as well as being commercial attractions. Many commentators have opted for hybrid explanations of the nature of town centres. Rannells, for example, blended elements of the bid rent, consumption and physical composition perspectives. He maintained that land use patterns were the product of a three-way relationship between accessibility – both in terms of goods and employees and consumers – availability of a suitable amount of space in the right location and linkages between businesses and also with customers (Rannells, 1956).

## The birth and evolution of town centres

We should not define town centres solely on the basis of their current composition, for they are continually evolving. Perhaps some of the ambiguity and disagreement about the meaning of town centres stems from the fact that many British towns have never had a single focal point, even when they were comparatively small. Many European towns of medieval origin contain central squares, places and piazzas, often fronted by important buildings such as town halls, churches and arts and cultural venues. Other functions such as markets and commerce congregated around such features but never displaced them. However, in medieval English towns, seats of government and administration, other civic buildings, religious and commercial functions were likely to be some distance apart. It would have been intriguing to inquire of the inhabitants of medieval Warkworth in Northumberland whether they regarded the centre of their town as the church as spiritual home at one end of the main street, the castle as point of refuge at the other, the site of the market between the two, or perhaps even the mid-point between church and castle. The multi-nodal character of British town centres also stems from the fact that markets were held in a variety of locations and not in central squares as was typical on the continent. They were staged along streets in most medieval towns which became lined with various guild halls and hostelries. In others, they were held in front of the castle gates or on cross-roads towards the edge of towns. This meant that the commercial activities were physically removed from civic, cultural and religious activities. In cities of great antiquity, the open spaces were as valued as the buildings since they fulfilled a variety of roles. They provided areas for public business, information and discourse – like the Greek agora and Roman forum – markets for agricultural produce and a stage for civic celebrations, processions and spontaneous events. Public spaces in

Britain on the other hand have not acquired the same significance and could be more easily eliminated when redevelopment occurred.

The physical separation of functions should not be overemphasised, however. Compared with modern town centres, the core of medieval English towns incorporated a rich mix of uses. This remained the case, despite subsequent expansion until the late Nineteenth century. They contained all the key civic functions, places of worship, cultural uses, commercial functions and most other forms of business. And the most influential citizens often lived there too. The main reasons for this mix of production, consumption, distribution and residential functions were convenience and safety. Centres of towns and cities provided a focal point for the exchange of goods and produce and maximum accessibility for its population. It was also common sense for the principal economic, political and civic functions and institutions to be located near to one another for ease of contact. Buildings in the centres of towns were also fortified to provide a last line of defence against hostile external forces. From the earliest times however, the size of urban settlements and the extent, nature and material wealth of their hinterlands dictated the diversity and importance of such functions. The main point about the concentrated, multi-functional character of central areas until the nineteenth century was that it bred a sense of solidarity, mutual interest and common endeavour despite the fundamental injustices of the feudal system.

The domination of town centres by retail and commercial functions is a comparatively recent phenomenon. Until the 1830s, the main streets of most towns were relatively peaceful except on market days (Girouard, 1990). Banks were often indistinguishable from private houses or shops which had simple glazed frontages. Specialisms were respected and competition scorned. Custom was secured by private invitation and display of wares rather than public advertisement. However, a combination of advertising, improvements in window display and use of architecture heightened competition and transformed the street-scene over the next century. Progressive refinements in glass manufacture enabled retailers to redesign shop fronts with almost uninterrupted window space. Coupled with the invention of the gas lamp and later electricity, and more sophisticated methods of display, this created the High Street we would recognise now. Expansion of newspaper advertising and circulation further fuelled demand for retail goods. Booming sales and demand for additional shop floorspace led to the development of arcades to exploit backlands behind the main frontages.

Successive developments in transport and telecommunications had a dramatic impact upon the appearance and composition of the High Street. The extension of distribution networks, combined with continuing restructuring of the industry associated with increasing competition, enabled multiple stores like Boots, Marks & Spencer and Woolworths to secure a strong foothold in provincial High Streets in the inter-war years. But a progressive concentration of ownership within the retailing and development industry, and the use of common architectural features and styles to project a conscious image, reduced the variety of the street scene. Whereas the nineteenth century High Street consisted of a melange of architectural styles reflecting diverse, local ownership of retail premises, especially after the Second World War, the retail environment was increasingly dominated and shaped by a few externally based retail chains which deployed similar mass construction techniques thinly veneered with their own corporate gloss (Whitehand, 1992).

The growing commercial significance of town centres had beneficial architectural consequences for town centres, at least initially. The end of the Bank of England monopoly in 1826 spawned the growth of joint stock banks as did increased advertising opportunities. They were joined by joint stock insurance companies from mid-century onwards and by building societies towards its close. Each sought to communicate in architectural language their reliability, dependability and wealth to attract new custom. Their buildings were invariably imposing, grand and opulent and were usually designed by the leading architects of the day in neo-classical, neo-gothic and renaissance styles. During the twentieth century, however, the design of all but headquarter buildings has progressively become more pedestrian, partly because of the concentration of ownership. During the period 1880–1940 several hundred local banks amalgamated into the big five (Martins, Lloyds, Midland, Barclays and National Westminster Banks). Also the development of safe and reliable lifts by the 1890s and the construction of steel-framed buildings shortly afterwards dispensed with the need for load bearing walls and literally made the sky the limit. This revolution in construction techniques later enabled developers to squeeze tall office blocks into increasingly popular town centre locations from the mid-twentieth century onwards. However, developers increasingly constructed on a speculative basis and minimised their risks by producing bland elevations of concrete and glass which contributed little to the streetscape and often lacked warmth.

Increasing demand for commercial space coupled with developments in public transport, particularly trams and the railways, led to the progressive depopulation of densely inhabited town centres. In the mid-nineteenth century there were still sizeable residential areas within most town centres. It was not uncommon for the head offices of joint stock banks located in a typical British High Street to contain a home for the manager (Girouard, 1990). Gradually, however, retail and commercial functions crystallised into the two principal elements of what have become known as central business districts. The advent of the railways, trams and then the automobile enabled the place of residence to be increasingly divorced from location of work. Moving out to the suburbs became a popular means of escaping pollution, congestion and other 'urban evils' from the 1930s, not just the privilege of the most wealthy. Commercial intensification, new road building and the expansion of public institutions, however, forced poorer groups into adjacent, increasingly crowded inner areas until they were 'rescued' by mass slum clearance and decanting programmes from the 1950s onwards. Manufacturing industry also decentralised from cramped edge-of-town-centre locations to cheaper, more spacious and easily developed sites in or beyond the suburbs.

Public policies accelerated the domination of town centres by commercial land uses for two reasons. Local authorities' ability to use compulsory purchase powers extensively in the 1960s and 1970s led to the comprehensive restructuring of town centres for retailing and office uses. Partnership schemes with developers resulted in a brave new world of enclosed shopping precincts, office complexes and pedestrian–vehicular segregation which cut swathes through the traditional fabric. Public provision of purpose-built industrial estates on the urban periphery and other parts of the built-up area eased the way for the decentralisation of manufacturing industry away from town centres.

In the 1980s, however, *laissez-faire* governmental attitudes concerning appropriate locations for development acted in precisely the opposite direction by weakening the town centres' monopoly of key commercial functions and major retail facilities. Waves of decentralisation of different forms of retailing, the advent of out-of-town business parks and leisure complexes, and continuing decentralisation of population and industry raised the possibility that town centres might revert to a more mixed pre-nineteenth century format. More pessimistically, they might also be progressively abandoned as has been the case in many US towns and cities.

## The role of modern town centres

In the light of their historical evolution what should we now assume to be the defining role and characteristics of the town centre? Clearly, their functional character has narrowed and their appearance has become increasingly similar due to increased external control of their assets. They have also come under sustained pressure from continuing decentralisation and competition from new centres. None the less they retain a variety of functions and have developed new indigenous strengths. There are three grounds for believing that many town centres could have a viable future and not prove to be dinosaurs.

*Economic diversification*

Town centres still possess traditional economic strengths such as accessibility and an ability to draw upon a large pool of labour. They are still regarded as the logical location for key decision-making functions and specialist retail and business functions serving extensive urban and regional areas. Some have tapped new markets. Large town centres are the launch pad for many product innovations and new types of producer services because of their large catchment population. Equally, larger centres are becoming major nodes for the exchange of electronic information and knowledge and are likely to be situated on information superhighways such as fibre-optic routes because of the number of local businesses and the frequent presence of higher educational institutions.

Growth in tourism, especially business and conference packages, city minibreaks and a growing interest in urban heritage has also opened up new opportunities for many town centres. Others have taken advantage of their geographical position by acting as gateways to their surrounding region. As a result, many town centres have witnessed a growth in tourism information bureaux, interpretative facilities, visitor accommodation and leisure and niche retailing attractions. Town centres also continue to be the focus of arts and cultural activity. Cheaper properties on the fringes of larger town centres have proved especially popular with the creative community who value the opportunity to mix with other artists, to work and live on-site and visit nearby arts and cultural attractions such as theatres, galleries and specialist retailers, which may be outlets for their work.

The town centres' importance in marketing terms has also grown. They contain the most notable and memorable historic buildings and spaces and convey powerful first impressions to visitors. They are frequently used as marketing devices to convey the distinctiveness and special qualities of a particular town, city or region. Many existing town centre institutions benefit from this additional visibility. 'Place marketing' adds to the symbolic significance of town centre locations and presents leading business interests with additional opportunities to use prominent town centre sites as a platform for projecting and publicising their own power and prestige. Environmental improvements, such as stone cleaning and greening, go hand in hand with such marketing in order to ensure that the reality matches the glossy image. Environmental attractiveness and a wide range of local amenities for employees are also recognised as being increasingly crucial to efforts to attract footloose domestic and international investors.

More speculatively, town centres may also benefit from the recent quest for more environmentally sustainable forms of economic development. Potentially they offer workspace which is widely accessible by environmentally benign modes of transport such as walking, cycling and public transport. Many recently developed employment locations can only be reached easily by car and cause additional congestion, pollution and severance.

*Enduring social and psychological significance*

Despite commercial pressures, town and city centres have the potential to perform a vital social and psychological role. They remain the focus of public events, festivals, street markets and meetings and contain the most important civic spaces and buildings. As points of arrival and departure, reunion and farewell, they evoke powerful memories. Despite the privatisation of public space, town centres remain the most important public domain for sharing communal and cosmopolitan values. They are places for promenading fashion, meeting, sharing personal experiences and broadening horizons with a central role in promoting social cohesion.

Increasing car ownership and a willingness to travel greater distances has tended to weaken the public's attachment to individual places. However, the sluggish housing and labour market throughout much of the 1990s, the growth of two career households and greater numbers of locally based small firms have counterbalanced this tendency (Dickens, 1988).

*Inertia and investment of capital*
Town and city centres are sustained by past commitments. Many retail, commercial, property owners and other interests have invested considerable capital in urban centres and cannot withdraw this capital immediately for legal and financial reasons. Public institutions like local authorities are equally committed to maintaining their role for employment reasons and to protect income from their real estate. They also seek re-investment on environmental sustainability grounds. To use existing urban assets in which society has already heavily invested makes more sense than creating new infrastructure on green field sites. Many public and private interests share a common interest in ensuring town and city centres' survival, at least in the short to medium term.

## The diversity of modern town and city centres

Each town centre has different strengths, legacies, challenges and difficulties. Their relative prosperity and social well-being is determined by a combination of size, the buoyancy of the local and sub-regional economy, spending power and behaviour of catchment population, degree of competition from neighbouring centres, quality of attractions, amenities and built environment, relative accessibility, levels of public safety, property ownership, land allocation and development control policies, land availability and the condition and degree of public–private co-operation, commitment and entrepreneurialism. Their prospects depend upon the dynamic interplay of property interests, retail and other businesses, custodians such as the local authority and amenity groups and their users including employees, customers, visitors and informal users.

Given this diversity and the methodological problem of gauging their character and health, the classification of town centres has proved difficult (see Appendix 1). However, URBED *et al.* have produced a classification on the basis of the main problems and opportunities town centres face (DoE, 1994). They identify three main determining factors: location, history and population and hence five major types of town centre:

- Free-standing market towns – usually of between 10,000 and 75,000 population with above average levels of affluence and car ownership which serve a rural hinterland and have developed incrementally.
- Industrial towns – of between 20,000 and 200,000 population which are prone to decline because of economic restructuring, loss of population and trade to neighbouring centres and the below average income of its residents.
- Suburban centres – are located within large metropolitan centres with a catchment population ranging from the very poor to the very wealthy depending upon the character of neighbouring residential areas.
- Metropolitan cities – have district populations ranging from 0.25-1 million and contain a wide range of functions, specialised quarters and important civic, cultural, social and commercial uses.
- Resorts and historic towns – with populations of 20,000 upwards whose economy is considerably dependent upon their tourism and heritage attractions and which contain a mixture of the affluent, the retired and people on low incomes.

This classification demonstrates that different centres experience problems to varying degrees. It is also a sensible way of applying good practice. But it downplays other factors such as size, users' views, wealth of the catchment population and institutional behaviour. Smaller town centres, for example, are particularly vulnerable to organisational restructuring within both public and private sectors to achieve economies of scale and savings in overheads. This has resulted in the widespread closure of smaller bank and building society branches and civic buildings in minor town centres. New superstores also inflict much greater damage upon the character of the High Streets of smaller towns because of their smaller number, and more limited range, of shops.

This book primarily focuses upon larger town centres with a district population of over 50,000 population, where there have been the most dramatic shifts in circumstances. It attempts to build an holistic and comprehensive picture of the dynamics of change but also identifies where general trends have had distinctive effects given varying local circumstances.

## Conclusion

In summing up, we inevitably return to the central question: what are town centres? The preceding discussion has suggested that there are different legitimate ways of seeing town centres. There is nothing immutable about their make-up. The last hundred years has witnessed the steady advance of commercial activities at the expense of social uses, only for town centres' role as centres of consumption to wane in the last decade and a half. They are arenas of conflict between private wealth creation and public spiritedness and places of compromise where the differing motives and expectations of their users must be reconciled. There is a constant tension between the desire for permanence on investment and psychological grounds and change and fluidity in order to maximise short-term profits. Most of all, town centres are a barometer of what is important to society as a whole rather than to collections of individuals because they are a crucial part of the public realm.

## References

Alonso, W. (1964) *Location and Land Use*, 16, Cambridge, Massachussets.

Bianchini, F. (1990) 'The crisis of urban social life in Britain: origins of the problems and possible responses', *Planning Practice and Research*, 5 (3), p. 4.

Christaller, W. (1966) *Central Places in Southern Germany* (translation by C.W. Baskin) Prentice Hall, Englewood Cliffs, New Jersey.

Department of Environment (1994) 'Vital and viable town centres: meeting the challenge', URBED *et al.*, HMSO, London.

Dickens, P. (1988) *One Nation? Social Change and the Politics of Locality*, Pluto Press, London.

Girouard, M. (1990) *The English Town: a History of Urban Life*, Yale University Press, New Haven.

Lynch, K. (1960) *The Image of the City*, MIT Press, Cambridge, Massachussets.

Rannells, J. (1956) *The Core of the City*, Columbia University Press,

New York.

Whitehand, J.W.R. (1992) *The Making of the Urban Landscape*, Basil Blackwell, Oxford.

## Chapter 2

# The retail revolution

### Introduction

Retailing has recently proved the most dynamic and most important town centre activity. Although town centres contain a variety of facilities and functions, most people go to town to shop. This, more than anything else, colours attitudes. This chapter examines recent developments in the retail industry, changing patterns of consumption and the evolution of government retail policy to assess their impact upon High Street retailing. It considers how the growth of new forms of retail investment in out-of-town locations has brought many town centres under increasing pressure and raised concern about their economic future. It tackles a series of questions. Has town centre former dominance of the retail sector been irretrievably broken despite recent government initiatives to tilt the balance in its favour? If it has, town centres will need partially to reinvent a role for themselves in order to remain viable in the future. To what extent have retailers and developers responded to consumer preferences by opening up new formats in alternative retail locations? What does this imply about the town centres' potential to lure back lost custom?

The chapter has three main sections. The first part identifies the profound changes in the nature of town centre retailing which have occurred in the last thirty years, and especially in the last decade. The second part weighs the relative significance of the restructuring in the retailing industry, changes in consumer preferences and evolving retail planning policy as motors of change. The final section speculates upon future developments in retailing which will affect town centres' destiny. The chapter concludes with an assessment of the overall implications of developments in retailing for the attractiveness of town centres.

## Major trends in retailing 1960–1995

Until the mid-1960s the distribution of retail activity was relatively stable. It assumed a hierarchical form ranging from local centres selling daily groceries and other convenience items to regional centres offering the entire range of goods. Most shops were concentrated within the most accessible central areas of towns and cities. Usually shops were small – there were over half a million in 1965 – and privately owned, although there were larger department stores selling a variety of goods and commonly occupying central positions within larger town centres. Customers tended to travel to shops on foot or by public transport and usually shopped several times a week. Since then, the scene has changed rapidly. Growth of disposable income, personal mobility, improvements in road infrastructure, decentralisation of population and economic activity and the changing practices of a few, increasingly dominant, retailers have transformed the nature and location of retailing. These changes have also affected the town centre retail environment, most notably producing shifts in the location of retailing, and changes in size and type of shop, external appearance and internal layout and in the style of customer service.

### *Growth of out-of-town retailing*

The dominance of town centre retailing has increasingly been challenged by the development of new free-standing retail facilities in more peripheral locations. There have been three distinct waves of retail decentralisation (Schiller, 1986). The first wave occurred in the 1970s. Free-standing supermarkets or hypermarkets of some 50,000–100,000 square feet with up to 1,000 car park spaces were developed, enabling more infrequent, bulk-buy shopping, mainly for food. Abolition of resale price maintenance in 1964 and the introduction of self-service had already paved the way for supermarkets to grow rapidly. Town centre congestion and land prices coupled with the size of such developments meant that stores were usually located on cheaper, more spacious, edge-of-town sites.

The second wave, in the 1980s, consisted initially of retail warehouses selling bulky goods such as furniture, carpets, electrical goods and DIY. These rapidly developed into better designed retail parks with leisure facilities and fast food restaurants, often selling a wider range of goods such as toys, shoes and sporting items. Again these were located mainly in peripheral areas close to existing food stores and/or on prominent, accessible sites, adjacent to ring roads and motorways. In 1980 there was only one suburban retail park; by 1992 there were 250. The final and potentially most damaging development has been the construction of vast regional shopping centres selling a full range of comparison goods and providing support services such as post offices and banks which were once the exclusive domain of the traditional retail centres. A key distinguishing feature of these schemes has been their initiation by developers rather than retailers, with substantial backing from investment institutions which were attracted by the 1980s boom in retailing and property investment generally. There were proposals for more than 50 regional centres in the late 1980s. To date, however, only a handful, like the Metro Centre at Gateshead, Meadowhall, Sheffield, and Merry Hill, Dudley, have materialised, mainly due to the recession or refusal of planning permission because of recent shifts in government retail policy.

This decentralisation of activity has had a major impact upon sales distribution. Between 1980 and 1991, the proportion of retail sales in out-of-town stores increased from under 5 per cent to 17 per cent (DoE, 1992a). Twenty-five per cent of shopping space is now located within out-of-centre stores (House of Commons Environment Committee, 1994). The number of shopping centres has expanded enormously, from around 190 in 1972 to 950 in 1994; but almost all the new ones have been developed outside town centres. Superstores and hypermarkets increased from only 21 in 1971 to 719 in 1992 – again, mostly located out-of-town.

### *Shop type and size*

The appearance of town centres has also been transformed by a series of internal forces. Perhaps the most tangible change is the way in which they have become increasingly similar in appearance, primarily because 25 retail groups trading under 200 brand names now dominate our High Streets. (Oxford Institute for Retail Management, 1990). In 1987 the top ten retailers accounted for 26 per cent of sales, and by 1994 the figure was 36 per cent (Corporate Intelligence, 1994). Corporate restructuring, mergers and acquisitions and vigorous competition for increased market share in the booming 1980s and the increasingly competitive 1990s have largely caused this concentration. Inevitably many smaller retail businesses have been edged out of central areas or put out of business. Between

1961 and 1984, the number of outlets fell by 36 per cent and the number of self-employed retailers almost halved to 300,000.

The reduction in the number of shops has been particularly marked in the grocery sector where the five largest supermarket chains now sell over half of all food consumed in Britain (TEST, 1989). Modest growth in sales of such convenience goods of only 15 per cent between 1963 and 1986 has resulted in cut-throat competition. This contrasts with the comparison goods sector where a dramatic growth in sales of 133 per cent between 1963 and 1986, arising from the development of new product markets, has offered scope for smaller specialised retailers to expand (Royal Town Planning Institute, 1988). Even in these sectors, however, small stores in existing town centres are under growing pressure because out-of-town superstore operators are diversifying their product ranges. Superstores have also attracted franchise operations and constellations of smaller shops which sell a wide range of comparison goods. Retail warehouse parks similarly contain stores selling goods which directly compete with those in town centres. Out-of-centre stores have also exploited the most profitable areas of growth such as DIY, gardening, furnishings and electrical goods. Verdict Research have estimated that £3 out of every extra £4 spent during the 1980s was spent in out-of-town centres (Verdict Research, 1993).

Many large multiples and supermarket chains have concentrated their activities in response to growing competition. In 1985/6, for example, the three leading food multiples opened 70 new stores but closed 232 in the UK. Smaller retailers in town centres have responded by moving into specialist niche markets like clothing, confectionery and stationery. In other more local centres they open for longer hours, and enter into federations to increase their buying power and protect each others' interests. However, competition from town centre multiples and out-of-town grocery superstores and retail warehouses has increasingly squeezed the margins of smaller retailers in town centres. Small shops are under particular pressure because the floorspace zoning system for rating purposes makes space for them relatively expensive unlike the large supermarket operators. Many smaller shops have to allow up to 10 per cent of their turnover for Uniform Business Rate payments.

Small operators have also come under increasing pressure for other reasons. The increased popularity of car boot sales has eroded their customer base and many claim to be the victims of unfair competition from charity shops who enjoy discounts on their rates.

The dramatic restructuring of the retail industry has had important physical consequences for town centres. Demand for larger outlets has promoted redevelopment schemes which favour large 'anchor' stores, often cutting across the previously finer grain of retail and other activities. Also, the property market in many town centres has become increasingly polarised between prime locations in demand from the large retail chains and increasingly downmarket secondary areas where smaller shops struggle to remain in business. This has produced marked differences in rental and leasing arrangements. Such changes have been mirrored by the increasing distinction between provision of superior quality convenience goods and some specialist retailing in core areas and discount provision interspersed with independent operators in more peripheral areas. The development of purpose-built shopping centres may have accentuated such patterns by shifting the centre of gravity and drawing investment away from more traditional areas. In many secondary locations during the 1980s, shops closed and were replaced by financial and leisure services operations such as banks, building societies, solicitors, estate agents, travel agents and restaurants.

It is perhaps worth noting that the concentration of control and improved efficiency of the retail industry has also had employment implications. Technological developments such as electronic scanning of goods and associated improvements in stock control have also raised productivity and lowered overheads. Whereas 2.3 million people worked in the retail industry in 1982, the number had shrunk to 2 million by 1994.

### *Design and appearance*

Retailers invest heavily in corporate image and marketing to boost sales. This involves frequent redesigning of shop fronts and internal refurbishment to reflect the latest fashions. But these changes can be disorientating and unpopular (Comedia, 1991). Concentration of ownership in a few hands has also reduced the variety of the streetscape and sense of place because of the standardisation of facades and logos in order to project corporate images. Frequently shop fronts are meretricious, failing to respect the local context because they are mass produced by externally based shopfitters. Purpose-built shopping malls emphasise the primacy of display space to the exclusion of all else because the driving pre-occupation is to maximise consumption and minimise potential distractions, although it must be admitted that more recent schemes have incorporated higher standards of landscaping and other uses. Often the external facades of such precincts are of mediocre design and appearance. Shop interiors have also become increasingly standardised and bland. Whilst store layout has become a fine art in order to maximise customer convenience, circulation and sales, relatively little attention is given to making the most of the architectural character of host buildings.

In the more marginal areas of town centres, frequent surrender and reletting of units or prolonged periods of vacancy lends such localities an air of impermanence which can be disorientating to shoppers and passers by. Such stores' tight profit margins and emphasis upon discounting and attracting bargain hunters means that quality of presentation and external design often suffers.

*Customer service*

The decline of the small shop and the tendency for many retailers to employ many part-time, poorly-paid staff without proper training, have resulted in the loss of a 'personal touch' which undermines standards of customer service. While major retail chains continue to hone customer services and aftercare, many other retailers now focus upon offering lower prices and keeping overheads to a minimum. This can, however, lead to the careless and slipshod presentation of goods and inferior customer care. Customers may tolerate this in return for the value for money shopping offered by out-of-town discount stores and warehouses. Town centre retailers face a difficult choice between matching such prices by deploying similar cost cutting measures and attempting to maintain their traditional strength in personal service which has proved so important in retaining customer loyalty in the comparison goods sector. Since overheads are greater in central locations it is essential for town centre retailers to emphasise the personal service aspect. But in the end their survival does depend on the willingness and ability of shoppers to pay a slightly higher premium in return. This high cost, high value added approach is more likely to succeed in relatively prosperous areas.

*Physical restructuring*

The physical evolution of town centres has closely paralleled the aforementioned changes. Five distinct phases of post-war retail development have been identified during which public authorities have closely collaborated with private sector retail interests (DoE, 1992).

- 1950s – Post-war reconstruction – to remedy the damage caused to many core areas by war time bombing and deal with associated problems such as interrupted frontages. In some instances, such as Plymouth, redevelopment did provide an opportunity to restructure part of the city centre and create a more spacious shopping environment.
- 1960s – Comprehensive development – which typically included the construction of purpose built centres containing large 'anchor stores', inner ring roads and multi-storey car parks on main access roads with the main intention of minimising pedestrian–vehicular conflicts.
- 1970s – Large scale, superior quality shopping precincts – of over 500,000 square feet and with more imaginative interiors e.g. Victoria Centre, Nottingham; Eldon Square, Newcastle.
- 1980s – Speciality centres which frequently entailed sensitive infilling with a mix of small-scale specialist outlets (e.g. Coppergate, York) and which sometimes contained a leisure component (e.g. Cavern Walks, Liverpool). This partially explains why over half of the mall developments catering mainly for specialist retailing were constructed in smaller centres outside the top 100 during that decade.
- Late 1980s – Refurbishment of earlier schemes to upgrade appearance, improve design quality and introduce fashionable uses such as food courts and leisure facilities, partly to counteract out-of-town competition. The concept of town centre management soon followed.

Some of the developments in the 1980s and 1990s have benefited town centres. Standards of design have risen, a greater mix of retail and other uses has been introduced and closer attention paid to customer needs through the introduction of crèches, better customer services, ramps for the disabled and leisure facilities. However, many town centres, through lack of public and private resources, are still coping with the physical legacy of 1960s and 1970s redevelopments. Often these were fundamentally flawed by poor design, overly-rigid zoning of retail uses, overemphasis upon shop fronts rather than other street and landscape features, and adoption of parking, vehicular and pedestrian circulation arrangements which proved unsafe and difficult to maintain.

Despite this, re-investment in town centres has recently taken place. Within larger town centres, major grocery chains such as Tesco are investing in high-density provision of basic 'top-up' goods. Such stores are also seeking to tap the growing market for convenience foods associated with increasing numbers of working women and single person households. Shifts in government retail policy in favour of town centres may also have encouraged such re-investment. More generally, progressive developers and retailers alike now realise that town centres' commercial success does not simply depend upon a healthy retailing sector. Visiting town centres is increasingly seen as a multi-dimensional experience involving shopping, cultural and leisure activities, promenading, eating and drinking and meeting friends. Consequently, recent town centre re-development schemes often contain a greater mix of activities than in the past, such as offices, cultural venues and residential accommodation as well as retail units. Such developments add to the vibrancy and appeal of town centres. Recent efforts to encourage the repopulating of larger town centres could, if they prove successful, further increase demand for local shopping facilities.

## The dynamics of change

Why have such major changes occurred? The explanation involves a combination of retailers' increasingly competitive behaviour, shifts in lifestyle and consumption patterns, local inertia and vacillating retail policies.

### *Competition for greater market share*

Retailing is an increasingly sophisticated, competitive and dynamic industry dominated by a growing number of international chains constantly in search of additional market share and greater profits. Retailers have many ways of achieving such goals. They include: marketing and promotion, adapting product ranges to shifts in consumption patterns identified by market research, price adjustment, increasing volume of sales, adding to floorspace, making cost economies, targeting goods at particular customers with changes in store format. Questions of optimal store location and size are integral to many of these strategies. Given a free hand, most leading retailers would now probably opt to concentrate provision either within existing town centres or new out-of-town retail parks. They would withdraw from suburban, district and local centres because of the growing distinction between 'destination' retailing and 'proximity' retailing. The former entails drawing customers from a wide catchment area by selling a wide range of quality goods at highly accessible and spacious locations, preferably situated out-of-town. Proximity retailing involves the sale of goods to meet immediate needs. Such shops are best located near concentrations of consumers such as town centres or major transport connections (Dawson, 1994).

Retailers and developers alike, increasingly prefer to develop out-of-town 'destination retailing' stores rather than within existing centres because they yield higher returns for two reasons. First, provision of retail space out-of-town is more straightforward and less costly. Lower land prices, fewer complexities of land ownership and property rights and less difficulty in accommodating the views of affected parties can avoid the delays and additional costs which tend to be decisive factors. Virgin sites also contain space to construct extensive flexible retail space on one level and provide extensive car parking. They are also easier to service. By contrast, retailers claim that most town centres are simply too cramped to accommodate modern store layouts. Upper floors, to which it is more difficult to lure shoppers, are also seen as a problem. Modern, single storey stores invariably achieve better sales per square foot figures. More generally, retailers have less control over environmental problems within town centres such as poor car parking facilities, crime, anti-social behaviour and eyesores than they do in out-of-town sites where such problems are less prevalent.

Second, out-of-town stores are located within areas of expanding demand because of the decentralisation of population and business activity and the personal mobility of more affluent suburban residents. The location of stores near to motorways and trunk roads also means that they can capture lucrative regional trade. The regional shopping centres have perfected such logic. Shoppers visiting the Meadowhall centre near Sheffield spend, on average, £50 on food shopping each visit compared with £10–20 in existing centres (Reynolds and Howard, 1994). Destination retailing also takes advantage of consumers' desires to maximise use of their leisure time by one-stop shopping, hence the growing product ranges of superstores. Longer working hours have made this doubly true. Adjacent leisure facilities have been provided for similar reasons. There is also a neighbourhood effect at work in out-of-town locations. Many of the more innovative developments in retailing over the last decade such as food superstores, garden centres, discount stores, and DIY centres have occurred in the vicinity.

Given the size of modern out-of-town stores and their potential regional catchment areas, a pre-emptive strike by one retailer can prove decisive in capturing trade, putting them in a virtually monopolistic position. The profitability of expanding the number of such outlets has hence led to a race – especially between grocery retailers – in which an inordinate proportion of the returns have been ploughed back into the development programmes rather than passed on to consumers in the form of lower prices (TEST, 1989). This has led to over-provision and saturation of the market. The decentralisation of retailing in the late 1980s and early 1990s induced a stampede effect amongst retailers. Those who would have been content to continue trading within existing town centres, from necessity rather than choice, had to consider opening up out-of-centre stores to pre-empt competitors capturing their trade. In spite of such pressures, many major retailers and institutions remain committed to town centre stores to retain their market share and protect existing investment. This accounts for the volume of recent refurbishment activity and retailers' support for environmental improvements and town centre management. However, if a retail chain opts to develop out-of-town within a static or slowly growing market, the chances are that it will either scale-down its town centre operations or close them altogether.

Growing competition, the race to develop new outlets, and increasing experimentation with new products to satisfy new tastes have had important consequences for the structure and location of retailing. They have invariably favoured the well-resourced large retail chains at the expense of the small, independent operator. Such concerns can use their sizeable profit margins or secure loan finance for development programmes, mount costly market research exercises on demand for innovatory new products, invest in new technology to cut labour costs and improve stock control, and use their buying clout to demand goods of the right specification at minimal price from manufacturers. Added to this, large stores gain many economies of scale, such as lower unit costs of renting floorspace, and their very size guarantees them preferential business and finance services.

*Shifting patterns of consumption*

The popularity of out-of-town retailing with customers and its success in commercial terms is indisputable. Retailers argue that this is not simply because out-of-town locations are more suited to modern retailing requirements but because they have successfully anticipated changing patterns of consumption. This section aims to show that the growth of out-of-town retailing and the decline of town centres is due to the complex interplay of different push and pull factors. Unavailability of data and lack of impact studies make it difficult, however, to assess to what extent loss of turnover in town centre shops is due to competition from out-of-town centres as distinct from other factors. Similarly, there is a tendency for the success of out-of-town centres to be judged in terms of trade and usage rather than assessing whether this is due to their intrinsic appeal or perhaps due to an absence of suitable shops and facilities within existing centres.

Push factors which have tended to discourage patronage of town centres and contribute to their decline include:

- A decline in the urban economy which leads to out-migration, reduction in the spending power of the catchment population and consequent fall in retailers' customer base and sales. Many traditional manufacturing and coal mining towns and coastal tourism resorts have suffered this fate.
- A dispersal of population and jobs and hence a growing demand for retail facilities on the urban periphery and in smaller towns in semi-rural areas.
- Environmental problems within town centres such as crime and anti-social behaviour, and eyesores such as litter, graffiti and the effects of vandalism, which undermine the overall quality of the retail environment and deter custom.
- A range of transport problems have made town centres less attractive to shoppers. These include under-investment in public transport, car dependence, poor car parking facilities and traffic congestion in addition to uninviting access points such as dimly lit multi-storey car parks and fume-filled bus depots and railway stations.
- An increasingly mobile urban population is able to reach a

much wider range of regional facilities and attractions, reducing the pull of town centres. This applies especially to the 25–44 age group.

- Many town centres have failed to move with the times. Standards of customer provision fail to live up to modern expectations and frequently differ from one town to the next. Shop opening times can vary and rarely cater for those who wish to shop after work. Facilities such as toilets, provision for the disabled and rest areas, which are increasingly in demand, are often found neglected or vandalised.

Pull factors include the following:

- The attractiveness of out-of-town centres because they sell an increasingly wide range of food and durable goods. This has been due to physical expansion in the number of shops and superstores' tendency to diversify their product ranges and make use of sales and storage space released as a result of continuing improvements in stock control.
- Out-of-town shopping centres which have been designed so as to reproduce the positive aspects of the High Street without their environmental drawbacks by providing a cleaner, safer, more accessible and more convenient shopping environment with leisure facilities for adults and children.
- Retailers have been adept at exploiting the growth of tourism and leisure by providing on-site retailing at tourist attractions or developing 'leisure retailing' attractions such as Albert Dock, Liverpool, where historic dock warehouses now house a mixture of shops and leisure uses. Garden centres and nature conservation and heritage attractions sell an increasing range of goods including books, household and outdoor goods and luxury goods. Such trends have promoted dispersal of retailing since most of these tourism venues are located outside traditional retail centres. For the mobile, there are now leafier attractions in which to spend leisure time and to shop than town centres.
- The growth in home-based, as distinct from social or community based, leisure pursuits has reduced patronage of town centres. The popularity of computer games, DIY and gardening has meant that more time is spent in the home and less in community pursuits. The fact that society is perceived as increasingly dangerous has reinforced the inclination to remain

at home or use neighbouring facilities and avoid journeying into the town centres, particularly at night.

- Customer values have shifted, partly because shopping has become a more individual experience and less of a social or community activity. The traditional appeal of town centre markets and personal service has consequently weakened while value for money, speed of purchase, ease of access and convenience, which are particular strengths of out-of-town shopping, are seen as increasingly important.

While it is easy to identify the strong push and pull forces which exist, it is difficult to isolate their relative significance. In deciding whether to alter their habits, shoppers have to weigh the advantages of patronising a new store with the opportunity costs foregone by no longer shopping at existing venues. The empirical evidence about why people shop and the appearance of the new regional shopping centres provide some useful insights into consumer behaviour. Studies of Merry Hill, near Dudley, the Metro Centre, Gateshead and Meadowhall, Sheffield, all show that shoppers liked their high quality of shopping environment especially the layout and sense of spaciousness, the ability to find most types of good under one roof, free car parking, shelter from the elements, the mix of retail and leisure facilities, their novelty and entertainment value and attractiveness as a day out (DoE, 1992b, 1993; Reynolds and Howard, 1994). Typically these centres appeal to the more affluent, mobile, middle aged family shopper. Clearly, higher levels of mobility and quality of transport infrastructure have been of crucial importance to the success of the out-of-town retailing phenomenon. More than 70 per cent of visitors to all three centres arrive by car from a catchment area up to an hour's drive time away, although day visits from even further afield are not uncommon.

Studies of such centres' impact on existing retail town centres have consistently revealed that the condition, status and proximity of the latter has crucially affected the volume of diverted trade. The centres which suffered most, notably Dudley and Sheffield, tended to have poor pedestrian environments and car parking and congestion problems. The least affected centres have been actively managed. They all possess an attractive retail environment, a good range of facilities and have the will and the means to remedy weaknesses and build on strengths. Although the Merry Hill study did not specifically address the question whether there was a need for a new centre, it did ask 1,500 households in Merry Hill's potential catchment area for their views on existing town centres. By far the most common response, mentioned by 42 per cent of the sample was the desire for an improved range of shops and retailers including the reinstatement of some who had left, followed by the need for better or free car parking (25 per cent), environmental improvements (10 per cent) and better facilities (5 per cent). Quite probably, Merry Hill has contributed to the most fundamental problem facing traditional centres by attracting some of their retailers and partially undermining many others, hence boosting its own relative appeal further.

Free-standing superstores or those located within retail warehouse parks are popular for similar reasons. They offer an increasingly wide choice of goods at reasonable prices enabling one-stop shopping, particularly for groceries, convenient car parking and general layout, and provide good support facilities such as toilets and play areas.

A strong reason for doubting retailers' claims that they are simply providing what the customer wants is that consumer preferences do not necessarily match retailers' priorities. Commercial considerations such as catchment quality, service charges, customer circulation, tenant mix and good management are uppermost in most retailers' minds. But cleanliness, pleasant environment and convenience from home matter most to the majority of shoppers (Courtney Research and Property Market Analysis, 1990). Other more dated studies have demonstrated the importance of price and quality of service, opening hours and overall design of shopping centres to consumers (e.g. Downs, 1970). Some commentators have suggested that the growth in leisure retailing and rising consumer expectations may engender public frustration with new retail developments' predictability, absence of a sense of place or historical continuity and lack of visual interest and excitement and their failure to accommodate ethical and environmental concerns (Newby, 1993).

### *Impact of government retail policy*

With the emergence of new forms of retailing, beginning with large free-standing stores and retail warehouses in the early 1980s, local and national government has faced the difficult task of framing retail policies which balance the needs of community access, existing shopping centres, relief of traffic congestion with a dynamic retail industry. In the last decade and a half the emphasis given to each of these factors has varied creating uncertainty and confusion amongst local authorities and the retail industry, and dramatic changes in the fortunes of town centres. Retail policy has passed through three phases.

*Conservatism*

Prior to 1979, retail policies were conservative in philosophy, preserving the existing hierarchy and protecting the status of town centres. The government's stance was encapsulated in Development Control Policy Note 13, 1977. This stressed the importance of town centres and sought to anticipate retailers' desire to construct free-standing superstores by declaring that such stores could only be built on edge-of-town sites where size, land requirements or some other valid reason prevented opting for a central site, and provided such developments did not damage inner areas. The need for new retail development was to be gauged using demographic and employment trends.

*Progressive deregulation*

However, this approach was flawed because only the quantity of retail floorspace was examined, not its quality. The possibility that existing floorspace was becoming outmoded either because of its nature, shape or location or because of new forms of retailing, was overlooked. The advent of the Conservative government in 1979 heralded an era when increasing recognition was given to the views of retailers and developers and less emphasis was placed upon regulation of retail provision. Circular 22/84 marked the beginnings of this policy shift by advising local authorities that they should not attempt to regulate competition between retailers or stifle new types of provision in out-of-town locations. Later advice became progressively more flexible culminating in Planning and Policy Guidance (PPG) Note 6 in 1988 which advised local authorities against prescribing limits for new floorspace and indicated that it was only necessary to assess the impact of large scale out-of-centre retailing upon the 'vitality' and 'viability' of the town centre as a whole. These concepts were vaguely defined in terms of the amount of vacant floorspace and range of services. But the cancellation of the Census of Distribution in 1981 precluded any meaningful impact analysis later. While there had been confusion and uncertainty about appropriate locations for retailing for much of the decade, it became increasingly clear that the government was more and more prepared to take a permissive line towards retail development in most locations except the green belt or where severe traffic congestion would result.

This drift towards a more deregulatory approach was doubly damaging to town centres. In the first half of the decade, town centre development was choked by a combination of restrictive and unimaginative local authority retail policies and a reluctant retail industry whose aspirations increasingly lay elsewhere and who sensed a change in central government attitude. During the late 1980s boom investment lagged because most local authorities followed the government's more permissive line on out-of-town retailing. They did so for varying reasons:

- Some welcomed the relaxation of controls as an opportunity to improve local facilities or generate more local jobs.
- Even those authorities traditionally opposed to out-of-centre retailing took a more pragmatic line because they feared losing development and jobs to neighbouring authorities who adopted a more relaxed attitude.
- Others favoured decentralisation to relieve congestion and protect amenities in historic centres.
- Worries that existing centres would be damaged by out-of-centre convenience stores and bulk retailing eased as it became clear that town centres' strengths lay in non-bulky comparison and luxury goods.
- Even if local authorities were disposed to refuse the application, they were reluctant to do so because if taken to appeal, they feared losing the case and having to award costs to the retail developer either because their Development Plans were out-of-date or because of inconclusive impact analysis.
- Out-of-town retail development proved a useful means of securing planning gain such as leisure facilities, car parks, access improvements and environmental works, using section 106 agreements.

Retailers' reaction to governments' deregulatory policies were mixed. Major operators, especially in the grocery and bulky comparison goods sectors, welcomed the opportunity to relocate in more spacious surroundings and the chance to tap new markets while established town centre stores were less enthusiastic and smaller retailers even less so. However, once the floodgates were open, those stores committed to trading in town centre locations were forced to open stores in out-of-town locations. Not to have done so would have been commercial suicide.

*Protective town centre policies*

Although the boom conditions of the late 1980s and *laissez-faire* retail policies offered a widening choice of retail formats in a range of locations, prolonged recession in the 1990s has increased awareness of the drawbacks of this approach. Despite some refurbishment within town centres and subsequent growth of speciality retailing, niche formats and 'leisure retailing', out-of-town investment had dwarfed town centre development in the late 1980s. During the recession it was plain that retailers were closing down or 'down-sizing' town centre stores to cope with associated shifts in consumption patterns and sluggish expenditure. Although an extreme case, a government sponsored study published in 1993 showing that Dudley had lost 70 per cent of its trade since the opening of the Merry Hill regional shopping centre became a *cause célèbre* (DoE, 1993). Similar evidence from elsewhere soon prompted the government to adopt a stricter policy stance towards out-of-town retailing. Worries about the compatibility of out-of-town retailing and the new concern for environmental sustainability, since out-of-town superstores generate large volumes of traffic and pollution, also provoked a change of thinking. Research had shown that a far greater proportion of people shopping in out-of-town centres travelled by car. By contrast, the location of large convenience/food stores in central locations accessible by public transport and the encouragement of local convenience shopping could play an important role in reducing transport emissions (TEST, 1992; DoE & DoT (Department of Transport), 1993)

In 1993, the government accordingly issued a revised version of PPG 6 which placed much greater emphasis upon town centres' importance in facilitating multi-purpose trips and minimising travel demand by providing a range of easily accessible services and retailing. Part of the guidance note addressed how town centres might improve their quality by diversifying land uses, improving accessibility and the pedestrian environment and appointing a manager to co-ordinate environmental maintenance, physical improvements and develop new attractions, undertake marketing and monitor performance. Much of the remainder of the guidance deals with new retail development. While it repeated earlier advice about not inhibiting competition and set out the reasons why larger retailers sought out-of-town locations, the revised PPG 6 did advise that the impact of out-of-centre retail proposals upon existing centres should be carefully assessed. Relevant criteria included:

- the proviso that all sections of the community should benefit from retail competition;
- availability of a choice of transport mode and avoidance of unacceptable increases in $CO_2$ and other pollutants;
- weighing the benefits of the proposal and its impact upon the viability and vitality of existing town centres in terms of:
  - future private sector investment needed to safeguard nearby town centres' viability and vitality;
  - quality, attractiveness and character of the centre and its role in economic and social life in community;
  - the physical condition of the centre and number of vacant properties in the primary retail area;
  - the range of services provided by the centre;
  - whether it would put at risk the strategy for town centres set out in their local plans.

The government later consolidated advice on how to reduce car reliance and the length and number of transport journeys, and encourage alternative means of travel by publishing PPG 13 on transport in 1994 in which shopping centres were again discussed. Broadly, the guidance recommended the promotion of retailing within existing centres able to offer a choice of access, particularly to those without a car, and more generally, the location of higher density development in areas accessible to alternative modes of transport to the car and minimal car parking provision.

Although PPG 6 and PPG 13 appear to hold out greater hope for town centres the reality is more complicated. For the next 2–3 years, the majority of additional development will continue to occur in out-of-centre locations because 60 million out of an estimated 96 million square feet of such development which is in the pipeline, with planning permission, is located out-of-town (Boney, 1994). In 1994, out-of-centre lettings amounted to about 16 million square feet as against under 5 million square feet in town centres. Existing out-of-centre retail locations will in any case further increase their market share both because local authorities are unable to constrain superstores from selling a wider range of goods and the tendency for a wider range of smaller stores to locate there making them relatively free-standing centres. Many retailers have indicated their wish to develop sizeable numbers of additional out-of-centre stores. Perhaps the stable door is being closed after the horse has bolted.

In the case of applications for retail development, the planning guidance is being variously interpreted by different parties, including planning inspectors. There is much evidence of confusion. While it is true that the higher rates of dismissal of retail applications by the Secretary of State for the Environment indicates that he is taking a firmer line, recent planning cases suggest that out-of-town sites can be developed in the following circumstances:

- If town centre interests are unable to assemble suitable redevelopment sites for financial, topographical or practical reasons.
- There is an inability on the part of the planning authority to demonstrate conclusively that demonstrable harm would be caused to existing centres by retail development, especially smaller stores whose cumulative impact may still be considerable. Tesco have responded to the guidance by developing more compact stores of around 20,000 square feet.
- Where out-of-centre retail development would strengthen the role of the nearby town centre by preventing diversion of trade elsewhere.
- Where out-of-town stores may reduce rather than increase trip distances and frequency such as recently urbanised peripheral areas.

Aspirations to boost retail investment in existing centres may also be thwarted by local authorities' inability to improve radically the town centre retailing environment and provide better development opportunities for retailers. Many have seen PPG 13 as a hindrance rather than a help because it counsels against the provision of additional car parking facilities which town centre interests argue are necessary to lure additional shoppers. Also, many existing centres struggle with problems which are not recognised in the guidance. Many shoppers would welcome greater variety in the size and nature of retailing but the guidance says nothing about how to reverse the continuing trend towards fewer outlets which is standardising the High Street and undermining its distinctive appeal. Megastores do not sit easily within town centres. The encouragement given by PPG 13 to home working or employment in such locations may also further emphasise the decline of existing centres.

## The future of town centre retailing

Although the recession has severely dented consumer confidence and dramatically slowed construction of additional retail floorspace, especially speculative schemes, the face of retailing will continue to alter dramatically. Given lower and more uneven growth in consumer expenditure, fiercer competition between retailers can be expected. Retailers will continue to experiment with new formats and products and target profitable niches and market segments. Since average incomes in suburban areas and small towns are expected to increase more than in inner areas and some outlying council estates, retailers will rationalise their existing store networks and open up new stores in expanding areas provided they can satisfy retail planning guidelines. Fewer retail chains will dominate the industry at the expense of independent, smaller retailers. Competition will intensify with out-of-town centres, and between town centres themselves.

Retailers will wish to expand in outlying retail warehouse parks, rather than invest in new town centre development. Alternatively, they may use the space saved in out-of-town stores by better stock control methods to diversify their product ranges. This creeping competition from the wider sale of comparison goods out-of-town, and the development of pharmacies and post offices on site, represents a steadily growing challenge to town centres. Out-of-town retailers are keen to target household durables and specialist goods such as clothing, sports goods, footwear and office supplies which are expected to generate higher than average sales growth in the 1990s. The liberalisation of Sunday trading laws also means that a greater proportion of trade will be secured by out-of-town stores since retailers have indicated they will concentrate on opening those stores which they believe will appeal most to family shoppers with cars.

Verdict expect sales growth of existing out-of -town stores to expand by 47 per cent by 1997, double the percentage rise of the trade as a whole, and the majority of an estimated 20 million square feet of additional floorspace to be constructed outside town centres (Verdict Research, 1993). They also predict that out-of-town stores will account for 33 per cent of sales by that date compared with 25 per cent in 1993 and 7.6 per cent in 1983. Even companies such as Boots which has devoted considerable resources to promoting town centre management, have indicated a strong desire to expand their store network into out-of-town locations. Such sobering predictions could partly be offset if the government responds to representations from town centre retailers and others to tighten controls on the range of goods and activities permissible in out-of-town locations (House of Commons Environment Committee (HCEC), 1994).

Town centre shops will also be vulnerable to competition from new retail formats, the majority of which will be located in out-of-town locations. One emerging form of retailing is the US-style discount warehouse club where limited ranges of a wide variety of comparison and convenience goods are sold at prices 25–40 per cent lower than those found in the High Street. The fact that they limit membership to professionals, business owners and civil servants enables them to offer discount prices in return for higher takings. While their regional appeal might lessen their impact upon individual town centres, a sizeable proportion of their customers may be private individuals and not wholesalers. They could therefore erode the market share of leading grocery retailers and other retailers selling electrical goods, office equipment and sports goods within existing centres. Although PPG 6 and 13 might limit the development of warehouse clubs in out-of-town locations, proposals on edge-of-town sites will be more difficult to refuse. Another format set to expand is the factory outlet centre, a grouping of factory shops where manufacturers sell mainly seconds and end-of-line goods, directly to the public at reduced prices. Clark's Village, Somerset, and Hornsea Village, near Hull are existing examples and 20 more centres have either applied for or received planning permission. The largest is the new 360,000 square feet out-of-town 'Cheshire Oaks' development at Little Stanney, Cheshire. Such developments could evolve into mainstream shopping centres selling general lines unless a firm line is taken.

In addition, town centres will experience increasing competition from home tele-shopping. Developments in interactive television and cable technology, and the appearance of consortia of retailers and telecommunications and media companies make this 'revolution' inevitable. While the importance of retailing as a social and leisure activity should not be underestimated, growing traffic congestion, crime and pressures upon time are going to make shopping a chore for many and will make fast, secure delivery of products to customers' homes increasingly attractive. On the basis of US experience of home shopping, High Streets could lose 20 per cent of their trade to computerised home shopping. Consumers will probably purchase goods from home which do not require inspection or where they can trust the retailer. Manufacturers may also use such media to undercut retailers' prices by selling direct to customers at wholesale prices.

These combined threats could result in significant retrenchment of town centre retailing. In addition, technological developments could further minimise space requirements. Greater use of VDU terminals for ordering convenience goods and customer use of wands to indicate a purchase will cut sales space and compensate for modestly increasing or static sales. Self-scanning devices utilising microchip technology are already being introduced to reduce queuing. Other possibilities include packing goods on the shoppers' behalf and home deliveries. While such trends may lead to the further contraction of most town centres' retailing area, the space released could be used for leisure pursuits such as eating, drinking, arts and cultural attractions. This might help town centres to offer a more interesting alternative to home shopping than out-of-town superstores and retail warehouse parks. The further introduction of new technology will, however, result in job losses.

If the predictions prove accurate, the future for town centres is quite bleak. They would increasingly serve only the needs of inner city residents and provide an ever lessening band of town centre workers with top-up goods and specialised products. Strict interpretation of new retail planning guidelines will be absolutely essential if town centres are to avert disaster. Their success in retaining business in the face of out-of-town retailing and tele-shopping will also depend upon whether they can make the town centre shopping experience more appealing than the alternatives and whether they can specialise in offering an impressive selection of interesting, distinctive goods or those requiring a high level of service.

## Conclusion

The rapidly changing face of retailing, shifts in consumer behaviour and the legacy of inconsistent and narrow retail policies pose immense challenges to authorities governing town centres. The flight of activity out-of-town and the polarisation of town centre retail property markets reflect societal trends such as disengagement of the wealthy from core areas and growing inequality. Similarly, the hegemony of retail chains at the expense of small locally owned shops has echoed the domination of small firms by large. All these factors cast doubt on the viability of town centres.

However, this dramatic reversal of fortune might have some advantages. It is over-simplistic to blame the retail industry totally for the decline of the High Street. There are many reasons for its demise. Changes in the distribution of urban population and economic activity and prospects, shifts in lifestyle and culture have all played a part. Neglect of town centres in policy terms and inconsistent, unclear and increasingly permissive retail location policies have prompted further haemorrhage of retail activity. A fundamental reappraisal of town centres' retail function and their management has long been overdue. Increased competition may force some authorities to consider novel ways of marketing town centres, such as using their architectural character and historic interest as an integral part of the consumption package. Many problems over the last decade have stemmed from the retail industry being given too much influence over consumption patterns, travel behaviour, energy consumption, access to facilities, environmental quality, residential location and job prospects. The dramatic transformation in the nature of retailing raises public policy issues which are too important to be left to a diminishing number of dominant large retailers driven by the necessity of achieving higher sales and profits.

The retrenchment of town centre retailing is already generating a healthy debate. If planning policies are successful in channelling future development into town centres, is another bout of development by a few megastores what is required or could it create more harm than good? In future, the mix in the size and nature of retailing units will need to be considered more closely in conjunction with other functions such as arts and cultural venues, leisure attractions, pubs and restaurants, the whole being properly integrated with residential and other social uses and commercial functions rather than hived off into monofunctional areas which die after closing hours. The current stagnation of town centre property markets may ironically enable greater intermixture of uses in the future if new leasing mechanisms can be devised and provided that local authorities are given a far greater stake in their town centres through relaxation of capital controls and reform of the rates system.

**References**

Boney, S. (1994) Speech to Belfast Chamber of Trade and Commerce, September. Reported in *Planning Week*, 2 (39).

Bromley, R.D.F. and Thomas, C.J. (eds) (1993) *Retail Change: Contemporary Issues*, UCL Press, London.

Comedia (1991) *Out of Hours: a Study of Economic, Social and Cultural Life in Twelve Town Centres in the UK*, Gulbenkian Foundation, Comedia, Stroud.

Corporate Intelligence (1994) *The Retail Rankings 1994*, CIR Publications, London.

Courtney Research and Property Market Analysis (1990) 'Survey of retailers in major new shopping centres opened in 1990', Courtney Research, London.

Dawson, J.A. (1994) *Review of Retailing Trends with Particular Reference to Scotland*, Scottish Office Central Research Unit, Edinburgh.

Department of Environment (1977) 'Large new stores', Development Control Policy Note No. 13, HMSO, London.

Department of Environment (1984) 'Memorandum on structure and local plans', Circular 22/84, HMSO, London.

Department of Environment (1988) 'Major retail development', Planning Policy Guidance Note No. 6, HMSO, London.

Department of Environment (1992) 'The effects of major out of town retail development', Building Design Partnership and Oxford Institute of Retail Management, HMSO, London.

Department of Environment (1992) 'Merry Hill Impact Study', Roger Tym & Partners, HMSO, London.

Department of Environment (1993) 'Town centres and retail developments', Planning Policy Guidance Note No. 6 (revised), HMSO, London.

Department of Environment and Department of Transport (1994) 'Planning and transport', Planning Policy Guidance Note No. 13, HMSO, London.

Downs, R.M. (1970) 'The cognitive structure of an urban shopping centre', *Environment and Behaviour*, 2, pp. 13–39.

House of Commons Environment Committee (1994) *Shopping Centres and their Future*, Report and Committee Proceedings, Vol. 1.

Newby H. (1993) 'Shopping as leisure' in Bromley, R.D.F. and

Thomas, C.J. (eds) 1993.
Oxford Institute for Retail Management (1990) 'Who runs the High Street?' Research Paper, OXIRM, Templeton College, Oxford and Bernard Thorpe.
Reynolds, J. and Howard, E. (1994) 'The UK regional shopping centre: the challenge for public policy', Oxford Institute of Retail Management, Templeton College, Oxford.
Royal Town Planning Institute (1988) 'Planning for shopping into the twenty-first century', report of the Retail Planning Working Party, RTPI, London.
Schiller, R. K. (1986) 'The coming of the third wave', *Estates Gazette*, 279 (6297), pp. 648-51.
TEST (1989) *Trouble in Store: Retail Locational Policy in Britain and Germany*, TEST, London.
TEST (ed.) (1992) *Travels Sickness: the Need for a Sustainable Transport Policy for Britain*, Lawrence and Wishart, London.
Verdict Research (1993) *Verdict on Out-of-town Retailing*, London.

# Chapter 3
# Choking to death

## Introduction

Town centres lie at the heart of extensive transportation networks which have always been their lifeblood. Commercial, retail and administrative functions have congregated in core locations because such systems offer easy access to a substantial urban and sub-regional population. Yet the economic and social well being of town centres is critically dependent upon the ability of residents and visitors to move around freely, cheaply, and in comfort without imposing heavy social and environmental costs upon others. It is increasingly difficult to reconcile the continuing demands for access to and from homes, workplaces, shops, leisure and social facilities of an increasingly car oriented society with urban quality of life. Paradoxically, alternative more environmentally benign modes, such as public transport and cycling, have declined in importance. Traffic congestion problems are the most frequently cited disadvantage of urban living in Britain and have become progressively more serious in town centres over the last thirty years (NEDO, 1988; Jones, 1991; Civic Trust, 1991). Many wish to move out of cities for this reason, although, ironically, this would add to overall traffic volumes. The future of town centres is going to depend upon how far transportation systems can support commercial activity without sacrificing environmental quality and decent living conditions. Commercial success or revival of town centres will ultimately prove self-defeating if they result in further congestion and pollution which will simply reinforce a deep-seated British anti-urbanism and lead to further decentralisation.

This chapter begins with a section describing the principal transport trends and problems affecting town centres. The second section explains why British town centres have become dominated by such an inefficient mode of transport when space is at a premium and estimates the relative significance of economic factors, social trends and personal preferences and government policy. The next section speculates upon future developments in transportation which could have a major impact upon town centres' prospects. The chapter concludes with a summary of the overall implications of recent developments in transportation for the quality of life in town centres.

## Transport in town centres

### *Growth in traffic*

Town centres, like everywhere else, have struggled to cope with an escalation in traffic. In Britain as a whole traffic volumes grew by 630 per cent between 1950–90 but expansion of road infrastructure failed to keep pace as road mileage increased by only 20 per cent (Association County Councils, 1994). Much of the increase in traffic has been due to growing car usage. In 1961 just under 60 per cent of the total distance travelled in Great Britain was undertaken by private car; in 1991 the figure was almost 90 per cent. By contrast, the proportion travelling by bus and coach dropped, in terms of distance, from 25–7 per cent and the proportion travelling by rail has risen only very slightly to 6 per cent. (Benwell, 1994). Vehicle ownership in Britain rose from 50 to 331 per 1000 persons in the period 1950–88. From 1981–91 the proportion of households with 2 or more cars increased from 26–42 per cent while the number without access to a car diminished from 22–13 per cent. Although the number of journeys has not increased markedly, there has been a pronounced increase in journey length. From 1961–93 the number of cars increased by more than 270 per cent while distance travelled increased by well over 300 per cent. Discretionary travel has increased much more rapidly than essential travel (DoE & DoT, 1993).

Town centres have been affected by traffic growth in different ways depending upon their population density, size and level of traffic restraint. Inhabitants in major urban areas travel less due to the greater concentration of employment and retailing in their city centres than those living in smaller cities and towns and especially rural areas. They also rely less upon the car because high population densities facilitate viable, cheap and reliable public transport and a greater proportion of residents either walk or cycle to local facilities or work (DoE & DoT, 1993; Kenworthy and Newman, 1989). In contrast to general trends, almost three quarters of those entering Birmingham city centre on an average day in 1991 used public transport and only 18.8 per cent a car. Some towns and cities, such as Oxford, Cambridge, York, Nottingham and Southampton have shown it is possible to encourage other modes such as cycling or taking a bus to the city centre because many of their residents travel comparatively short distances. Generally, however, car use has increased at the expense of other modes within most town centres.

*Counting the cost*

'Cars come gift wrapped in sex, freedom, potency, money, glamour and individualism' (Sawyer, 1994). But they are ruining our towns. The personal benefits of car ownership such as convenience, flexibility and door-to-door access are heavily offset by community costs, especially in town centres. Four negative effects may be distinguished: lack of space and economic, environmental and social costs.

*Too many cars, too little space*

Cars have consumed scarce and valuable central urban space in an alarming, unsustainable fashion. Town centres have been particularly vulnerable to growth in traffic and car ownership. Part of the problem is the uneven incidence of traffic movements. Over 40 per cent of all traffic occurs within built up areas and over a third of urban traffic is at peak periods (07.00–10.00 and 16.00–18.00). In Manchester, a 13 per cent increase in peak hour traffic in recent years has increased journey times on radial routes by 33 per cent (Howard, 1991a). But the principal difficulty is lack of space. The 14 per cent of London's commuters travelling to work by car already account for nearly 85 per cent of the road space. Conveying one person by car consumes 50 times as much space as if that person had used public transport and 20 times as much as use of a bike. One employee's car parking space occupies a surface area equivalent to that of his own office (Howard *et al.*, 1991b).

Since there is limited scope to expand transport space within town centres, engineers have faced a difficult task accommodating cars, and catering for public transport, pedestrians and cyclists. Burgeoning car usage has made it more difficult to reconcile the demands of businesses, commuters, shoppers, residents and visitors. Pedestrianisation has been one response but elsewhere pedestrians still risk injury from vehicles. They also have to negotiate an obstacle course of lamp posts, signs, grit boxes, bollards and railings. Cyclists rarely enjoy dedicated roadspace and risk serious injury from cars, lorries and buses. Transport planners also have to take into account broader land use conflicts and commercial considerations. Pedestrianisation proposals are frequently opposed by traders because they fear they will lose custom. Even the location of bus stops and taxi ranks can be a matter of life and death to retailers.

### *The economic costs of congestion*

Traffic congestion is the most tangible result of the incapacity of existing transport networks to handle additional traffic. Accidents, road works, breakdowns, illegal parking and wheel clamping can cause further disruptions to flow. The concentration of activity and historic buildings in central locations complicates the attempt to modernise infrastructure. Shortage of ground-level car parking and high land values led to the development of multi-storey car parks which have often proved unpopular with cautious drivers and those vulnerable to personal attack. Even better designed, well-lit and managed multi-storeys create problems because their popularity generates further congestion. Servicing town centres is increasingly problematic because of delays caused by congestion and because many town centre streets are too narrow to accommodate large lorries. This has prompted some local authorities, especially in historic town centres, to provide transhipment centres on the outskirts from which smaller goods vehicles transport goods into centres. But they add to transport costs.

The economic consequences are severe, particularly for businesses. Failure to deliver goods on time, missed appointments and the general waste of time, loss of energy and extra depreciation because of delays all add to costs. The Confederation of British Industry has estimated that congestion costs the British economy £15 billion a year adding £10 per week to the average household's cost of living (CBI, 1989). Now that town centre retailers use 'just-in-time' methods of stock control and delivery to display a wider range of goods, delays may result in significant lost revenue.

Congestion has led to the wider commercial decline of town centres. City centre employers have become increasingly reluctant to bear the consequences of traffic congestion and have decentralised their operations. This may ultimately generate additional travel demand. But this is offset, initially, by higher travel speeds and reduced journey times. Congestion also limits the viability of public transport. Additional traffic lowers public transport speeds more than car speeds. During peak conditions within London, cars average 11 mph whereas buses average only 5.5 mph. Slower journeys and deteriorating standards of service lower passenger numbers. Public transport operators are forced to respond by increasing the frequency of service which leads to higher costs. Dissatisfied customers then switch to cars and increase congestion, further reinforcing the downward spiral.

*Environmental impact*

The environmental impact of traffic growth has provoked enormous worries since transport emissions are responsible for generating a cocktail of dangerous pollutants with serious potential health hazards (see Royal Commission on Transport and Environmental Pollution, 1994). There is growing scientific evidence of a link between vehicle emissions and asthma, other respiratory conditions and cancers. Road vehicles in Britain account for 20 per cent of $CO_2$ emissions, the principal greenhouse gas, 90 per cent of carbon monoxide, 50 per cent of nitrogen oxides, the majority of lead pollution and 46 per cent of black smoke (UK Quality of Urban Air Review Group, 1992). These percentages rise markedly in urban areas and are even higher within busy town and city centres, especially at rush hour times. Weather conditions such as temperature inversion can trap these pollutants so that poisonous photochemical smogs can hang over cities for days. While there is little comprehensive research on the health risks of pollution in town centres, the levels are probably dangerously high. EC safety limits for emissions of $SO_2$ and $NO_2$ are regularly exceeded in Edinburgh city centre, for example. Only in pedestrianised areas and enclosed shopping precincts is there partial escape from the pollutants.

Although the automobile industry has responded by introducing catalytic converters, better fuel quality and low-emission engines, the impact of such technical innovations has made little difference. Growth in traffic volume has offset lower emissions. More seriously, old or poorly maintained vehicles can produce 40–50 times the amount of pollution from the cleanest cars. The principal offenders are old lorries, taxis and delivery vans and the increasingly ageing bus fleets of public transport operators, where low operating margins and lack of investment prohibit fleet modernisation (Holman, 1992). A survey by the Society of Motor Manufacturers and Traders (SMMT) revealed that over 60 per cent of buses and coaches in service at the end of 1993 were over ten years old (SMMT, 1994). Deregulation has meant more operators and more buses in major town centres, further worsening air quality. There are currently 27 operators in Liverpool!

Increases in car commuting make pollution levels even worse. Though modern cars are fitted with catalytic converters, they do not work to full effect over short distances of up to 2.5 miles when the exhaust is warming up – they screen out only 75 per cent of emissions at this time as against 90 per cent at full efficiency. The increased use of diesel cars has also proved a mixed blessing. Unlike petrol cars without catalytic converters, they emit only minimum levels of benzene – a known carcinogen – and produce less carbon dioxide even than petrol cars with catalysts. But most emit similar levels of nitrogen oxide and higher smoke levels in the early years of their life with greater concentrations of harmful substances such as polycyclic aromatic carbons which some researchers claim are more mutagenic than petrol car emissions. Congestion also wastes energy. An estimated 25 per cent of all fuel used in urban areas is consumed by vehicles while they are stationary (DoE & DoT, 1993). Car dominance makes matters worse since on average, they consume about three times more energy per passenger than buses and trains (Commission of the European Communities,1992).

### *Social impact*

The social damage caused by increased car usage is serious. As traffic volumes have grown, more space has been given to roads and car parks, especially in inner residential neighbourhoods, progressively eroding home territory (Appleyard, 1981). The loss of housing, local shops, social facilities and open space because of highway construction, as well as parents' worries about busy roads, have led to decentralisation of population and jobs and increased car dependency. This has accentuated disparities in access to employment, retailing and leisure opportunities. The affluent and mobile are relatively well placed. But those without access to cars within inner areas are increasingly disenfranchised since they cannot afford rising public transport fares and have to rely upon run-down local facilities and stretched social services.

Local traffic levels make town centres and neighbouring inner areas less attractive places in which to bring up a family. As vehicle flows increase, pedestrian movement and street bustle and activity diminish. This reduces natural surveillance and presents additional opportunities for criminal activity. Residents' concerns about safety on the streets means they increasingly use the car, even for short distance journeys, further reducing pedestrian safety. Car domination also restricts healthier forms of travel such as walking and cycling because of the attendant risks. The rate of deaths and serious injuries per mile travelled is estimated to be 14 times higher for cyclists than for motorists (Morgan, 1991). Fears of crime and road accidents have prompted many parents to escort their children to and from school by car. But this, in addition to increasing congestion, has led to a loss of physical exercise and may have inhibited children's road sense, self-esteem, identity and ability to develop coping skills (Hillman, 1993).

## Reasons for car dependency

Why have cars been allowed to dominate town centres? In theory, priority might have been given to transport which uses space most intensively and to tax and subsidy levels which reflect the real costs of different modes. This section explains why this has not happened.

### *Growth in mobility*

Increasing traffic characterises the most economically advanced societies. The continuing revolution in transport and telecommunications and the development of global financial systems has enabled companies to compete and trade in global markets. Individual, family, cultural and business horizons have also expanded. Widely available, relatively cheap motoring has broken the link between home, work, retailing and social and leisure facilities. Rising car ownership has enabled commercial and retail interests in town centres to decentralise their operations to more peripheral areas which are not as accessible by public transport and to transfer transport costs to the consumer or commuter. As a result, car ownership has become a necessity rather than an option. Increased personal mobility has exposed town centres to increasing car congestion and competition from other towns and new centres of commercial activity on the periphery. Dispersal of population has diminished the viability of public transport and led to an increased number of car-borne trips into town centres. Factors which have contributed to increased personal mobility and greater volumes of traffic are summarised in the table below.

**Table 3.1: Forces encouraging increased mobility**

Economic factors:

- globalisation, decentralisation and specialisation of production
- relative decrease in transport costs
- increased size of production, distribution and retailing outlets to achieve economies of scale and pass transport costs onto the consumer
- advances in telecommunications which have facilitated decentralisation of routine office functions
- growth of out-of-town retailing, warehousing and business parks
- growth in bulk-buy shopping
- increasing demands for delivery of goods at short notice – 'just-in-time'
- growth of sub-contracting and hence service industries which require increased contact between customer and provider
- widening areas of job search
- preference for suburban, semi-rural residential locations leading to increased separation of home from work and journey to work times
- higher real incomes and increased affordability of cars
- increased ability to choose between competing leisure, shopping and other functions
- increased range, volume and sophistication of consumer goods
- increased necessity of car ownership given diverse and growing pressures upon personal and family time

Social and cultural influences:

- more dispersed kinship, friendship and social networks
- increasing number of single person households and childless couples
- growing numbers of working women
- the related growth in two income, two car households
- increasing size but diminishing number of public services such as hospitals and schools
- the status value consumers attach to cars
- associated values relating to personal freedom and mobility
- growth of leisure time and expenditure
- increased number of leisure, tourism and arts and cultural attractions accessible only by private cars.

*Source*: based on DoE & DoT, 1993

The catalogue of factors listed in Table 3.1 still does not adequately explain why car usage has increased in town centres at the expense of walking, cycling and public transport which are so much more space-efficient and environmentally friendly, more economically viable, traditionally popular and less socially destructive. Many European towns and cities have a dispersed form and high levels of car ownership but have fewer traffic problems because alternative modes are popular. A range of evidence suggests that there have been failings in transport policy which have played a major part.

*The policy vacuum*

Despite recent policy changes, government transport policy over the last decade and a half has favoured cars at the expense of other means of travel. Since 1979 the Conservative administration has tried to inject greater competition into the transport industry to improve efficiency, reduce subsidies, foster individual choice and encourage innovation. However, road transport has not been fully exposed to market forces. Taxation structures, investment criteria, subsidy levels and project appraisal methods favour road rather than rail investment and car usage rather than public transport. The government's philosophy has been to accommodate growing road freight and car usage by spending on road construction, and better transport management such as the computerisation of traffic signalling and more sophisticated car parking controls rather than restrict the demand for travel and influence choice of respective mode so that existing infrastructure is used in a more environmentally acceptable way. Although the policy has been to minimise conflicts between motorists, pedestrians and cyclists through safety measures, segregation, speed limits and public education, there has been no serious restriction on the motorist.

This general approach is completely inappropriate to town centres since there is little scope to add to existing infrastructure because of lack of space. Continuing emphasis upon road building elsewhere has generated additional urban traffic. A recent report has shown that road building exacerbates rather than alleviates congestion by generating additional traffic (Standing Advisory Committee on Trunk Road Assessment (SACTRA), 1994). Despite Colin Buchanan's prophetic warning over thirty years ago about the impossibility of accommodating projected growth in vehicle traffic without restraining traffic or restructuring core areas to separate roads, car parking and pedestrianised areas, neither approach has been adopted. National and local government have ducked the implications of rising personal mobility because of the strength of public opposition to comprehensive redevelopment plans in the 1960s and financial constraints in the 1970s and 1980s. Congestion has not generally been anticipated by technical solutions such as localised travel information, vehicle guidance systems and traffic control systems. Since the rejection of pedestrian–vehicular segregation and construction of urban ring roads, a visionary approach to urban transport policy has not emerged. Government has essentially muddled through, and often made matters worse.

### *Coughing up for car owners*

Motorists are fêted in town centres despite the problems they cause. Developers insist that commercial accommodation must have enough car parking to make them more marketable. Off-street car park charges do not cover capital and operational costs. Local authorities are offering discounted rates to lure back car-borne shoppers from out-of-town locations. Even when fined for illegal car parking, motorists' charges do not cover police administration and enforcement costs. Most significantly, road users are not charged fully for the costs of road construction and maintenance nor do they cover the environmental costs of noise, vibration and air pollution. Discounting motor taxes, each motorist is subsidised by £1000 per car per year (Transport 2000, 1994). Although government rules on company car taxation have been tightened to penalise high fuel consumption, they remain extremely generous. Company car owners drive extra distances because they can save up to £600 a year by crossing tax thresholds of 2,500 and 18,000 miles of business mileage. Such motorists drive an average of 5,000 miles more each year than those who own their own vehicles. Since company cars represent over half the cars on the road, their impact upon town centre congestion is enormous.

The government's stance is rooted in ideology, short-term accounting and vested interests. Growth in car ownership is seen as a barometer of wealth and personal freedom. But it also generates vast revenues from fuel and vehicle taxes far exceeding government expenditure on transport (Buchanan, 1988). Also, the road construction and car manufacturing industries are strategically important to the British economy and a powerful lobby group with strong links to the Conservative Party. Consequently, government has placed its faith in industry's technical solutions to congestion and pollution rather than resorting to controversial policies restricting vehicle usage.

*Lack of government support for alternative modes*

While car manufacturers have spent millions on improving car technology and performance and cabin comforts, government investment in public transport and other modes has fallen drastically. This is partly because the rules governing investment in new rail and bus rolling stock and infrastructure are more stringent than those for additional roads. But it is also a result of cuts in subsidies since 1981 and deregulation of bus services outside London. Although deregulation enabled the Treasury to reduce exchequer contributions to public transport, services became expensive and unreliable as levels of maintenance and replacement of stock fell (Howard, 1991a). Operators vied with one another on the most popular routes and produced additional congestion. Greater Manchester's experience is typical. Bus patronage in the period 1983–86 was 350 million journeys per annum. After deregulation the figure fell to 290 million. While some passengers transferred to rail, most switched to cars.

Fare rises caused by reductions in subsidies have made motoring appear a more attractive option. Before 1981–91 bus fares rose over 100 per cent while motoring costs rose by only 59 per cent. London Regional Transport now has to cover 90 per cent of its operating costs by commercial revenue. In Paris, only 40 per cent of expenditure is covered by fares. Thirty-two per cent of expenditure is covered by state allowances split between state and region and employers contribute 24 per cent of the cost. Fares in London are the most expensive in Europe and twice the average fare levels in other European cities (London Research Centre, 1992).

In the face of falling patronage, fare increases, declining catchment population, lower travel speeds and the location of major traffic generators away from public transport routes, operators have only remained profitable by cutting maintenance budgets and extending the service life of buses. Abolition of the bus grant in 1984 which allowed bus operators to claim 50 per cent of the purchase price of new buses from government has also increased the average age of vehicles. Ageing fleets have undoubtedly contributed to the downward spiral of passenger numbers because of their poor image, greater exhaust emissions and increased unreliability.

This position is mirrored on the railways. Total subsidy levels as a proportion of overall costs were only 18 per cent in Great Britain in 1989 compared to 41 per cent in West Germany, 45 per cent in the Netherlands and 52 per cent in France. National expenditure on rail infrastructure in 1991 was 9.9 million US$/capita compared with 31.9 million in Germany, 31.4 million in the Netherlands and 54.4 million in France. Government revenue support for Network South East fell by 55 per cent from 1985 to 1989 and further cuts have followed. Rolling stock on the network now averages 19 years old. Punctuality is poor, customer satisfaction is plummeting and worry about maintenance and safety standards is growing (Steer Davies Gleave, 1992). Great Britain now ranks bottom of the European public transport league on all the key measures.

Cycling and walking have been neglected by national government and locally except in a few enlightened local authorities. Provision reflects the distances travelled by different modes, and therefore favours the car (Tolley, 1990). While 2 per cent of personal journeys are by bicycle, expenditure on cycling facilities in 1987/88 was £160,000 as against £900 million for the national road programme. Declining cycle usage – down 30 per cent from 1981 and 1991 in

London, for example – partly explains this modest level of resources, but this is more a reflection of increasingly hazardous road conditions rather than a decline in the popularity and potential of cycling. In 1988 cycling conditions were reported as the worst in Europe outside Belgium.

Although some local authorities have adopted more positive attitudes towards alternative modes, they are the exception rather than the rule. Central government financial support to local authorities has been lacking and local revenue raising powers are limited. There has been a fragmentation of control caused by deregulation and the abolition of metropolitan-wide authorities. The recent award of £42.5 million of national lottery moneys towards the cost of a 5,000 mile national cycle network designed by the charity Sustrans, which will require a total investment of £250 million to complete, is good news but such a project should have been funded by the government years ago.

*Underinvestment in transport infrastructure*

Local authorities have also faced difficulties accommodating increasing numbers of cars. Construction of new car parks has been hampered by public expenditure controls and Treasury restrictions upon local authority use of capital receipts as well as strict time limits upon the disposal of compulsorily purchased land. This has deterred local authorities from acquiring land and entering into partnership ventures with the private sector. Town centre locations are particularly problematic because high land and property prices and logistical difficulties associated with cramped working conditions add to costs. A town centre multi-storey car park costs as much as £4 million to develop. Car park receipts do not fully offset overheads and many hard pressed local authorities, rather than putting the revenue into maintenance and improvement of transport infrastructure, have raided it for other purposes.

Many town centres still live with the mistakes of the 1960s such as underpasses and insecure multi-storey car parks and lack the resources to remedy them. Customers prefer clean, well equipped and non-threatening environments to poorly maintained, run down and unwelcoming bus and railway stations and multi-storey car parks.

*Rejection of land and transportation planning*

The management of urban areas has always required a local understanding of the relationships between land usage, travel patterns and different forms of transportation. Locating major traffic generators near to public transport routes has been particularly crucial in town centre locations because of the need to maximise passenger flows and exploit the limited space. Yet during the 1980s, such strategic planning was seen as holding back development and fell out of fashion. Planners were exhorted to let developers build in a much wider range of locations including out-of-centre sites which were poorly served by public transport. This deregulatory approach has produced congestion and car dependency and diminished the viability of public transport.

*Fragmentation of responsibility*

Achieving integrated land use and transport planning has become even more difficult as a result of bus deregulation. The multiplicity of public transport operators has complicated Passenger Transport Executives' task of integrating different forms of transport in town centres and planning infrastructural improvements. Transport planning has never been easy because responsibility is split between different departments and tiers of government. County and District Highway Authorities and the police together formulate highway and car parking policies which has slowed down the reform of circulation arrangements. Within individual local authorities, planning departments have pressed for greater pedestrianisation and traffic restraint while engineering departments have focused upon maximising traffic flows. Within central government, the Department of Transport and the Department of Environment have differed over priorities for public and private transport.

Cars do have a powerful appeal to individuals but government policies have reinforced personal preferences. As Table 3.2 shows, private transport offers advantages in terms of flexibility, personal safety, convenience, comfort and status. Also, once the fixed costs of vehicle purchase, road tax and insurance are met, the perceived cost of motoring is often seen as merely petrol and parking. Company mileage allowances, free parking at out-of-town retail centres, credit cards, etc. create the illusion that the trip is almost free. Public transport, on the other hand entails waiting and uncertainty, perceived added danger and an immediate cash outlay unless one has a travel pass. The poor image of public transport has emphasised the gap. The degree to which people are wedded to their cars will have serious consequences. Hallett, for example, has shown that over 60 per cent of car users and 40 per cent of less frequent users would not change mode even if congestion doubled their journey time (Hallett, 1990). This inflexibility in travel behaviour suggests that congestion could reach crisis proportions before people see the wisdom of using other means of travel.

**Table 3.2: Public transport and personal preferences**

| Constraints of public transport | Individual preferences |
|---|---|
| Mass transport | Individual tribal transport |
| Homogeneity and indifferentiation | Marginal differentiation, personal expression |
| Dull | Exciting |
| Exposure to risk (single person buses, unmanned stations) | Privacy, safety |
| Fixed itinerary | Flexible itinerary |
| Authority, formality (inspectors, timetabling) | Freedom, autonomy |
| Low social standing | Fashionable |
| Low innovative content | High innovative content |
| Unreliable | Reliable |
| Spartan | More comfortable |
| Realistic | Escapist |

*Source*: based on Laconte, 1992 .

However, some surveys have shown that a significant proportion of motorists would be prepared to use public transport if it was available, fast and reliable (Jones, 1991). Car dependency persists because of the lack of a good alternative rather from choice. Attitudinal studies show rather more support for policies that increase choice of mode but a cooler response to policies which restrict personal use of the car, especially road pricing (Which, 1990; Hallett, 1990; Pharoah, 1992). If these surveys are representative, national and local government have a crucial job, in reshaping public travel behaviour. They have failed to rise to the challenge and most of the blame for this must rest with central government.

## Prospects for town centre transport

The extent to which transport systems ensure the flow of goods and people will depend upon socio-economic influences, travel demand, vehicle ownership, land usage and transport policy. The government's own projections suggest that town centres will have to cope with dramatic increases in demand for movement because past trends are expected to intensify in future. National Road Traffic Forecasts predict a possible further 50 per cent increase in the demand for movement within the next twenty years. Government estimates also suggest that car traffic could double over the next thirty years (Royal Commission on Transport and Environmental Pollution, 1994). The number of cars is also set to rise from 19.7 million in 1989 to about 25 million by 2,000 – an increase of 20–30 per cent. If these estimates are correct, vehicular ownership will rise from 330 cars per thousand in 1989, to between 385 and 430 by the turn of the century.

Future travel patterns will also depend upon town centres' relative attractiveness in commercial and environmental terms and broader patterns of urban development which will affect car dependency and the viability of public transport. However, the interrelationships between increasing the size of facilities, the decentralisation of commercial activity, population densities, new out-of town centres and attractions and the volume of traffic in different locations, including town centres, are at present improperly understood. In addition, since town centres are able to accommodate only modest additional traffic anyway, management of both infrastructure and traffic demand will be crucial.

There is a growing consensus amongst academics, professionals, politicians and the public that worsening traffic congestion and environmental problems require a fundamental change of attitude to cars. Supply of road infrastructure cannot possibly keep pace with demand. As well as better traffic management and land use planning, improvements in public transport, advances in technical efficiency and development of alternatively powered cars, traffic restraint measures will be an absolute necessity. Revisions in planning guidance reveal a shift in government thinking. PPG 13 on planning and transport seeks to minimise emissions by reducing the length and number of motorised journeys and lessen reliance on private cars (DoE, 1994). The guidance recommends a set of measures including:

- channelling development in urban areas where there is a choice of mode including public transport;
- the closer juxtaposition of employment and residential uses;
- intermixture of retail and leisure and entertainment uses;
- location of superstores on edge-of-centre sites accessible by foot.

The guidance also recommends that traffic calming measures, intended to reduce vehicle speeds, are preferable to additional road investment if they are supplemented by:

- better public transport provision;
- parking controls;
- better traffic management;
- improved networks of cycle routes;
- possible road pricing.

To encourage this to happen, central government is inviting local authorities to submit 'package' bids to attract resources for initiatives integrating different modes of transport.

A recent report has gone further recommending a virtual abandonment of the government's road building programme and rechannelling the money into public transport (Royal Commission on Transport and Environmental Pollution, 1994). The publication of the SACTRA report which argued that road construction generates additional traffic also signalled an end to an unquestioning acceptance of the economic case for investment in roads.

But, although PPG 13 contains the right messages about traffic restraint, reducing car reliance and encouraging more environmentally friendly transport, translating such principles into practice will be seriously undermined by the government's own transport policies. Although better land use and transportation planning will reduce the need to travel and concentrate investment in town centres, the effects will only be felt in the medium to long term because only 1–2 per cent of the built fabric is renewed every year (DoE & DoT, 1993). Despite the private sector's poor record on investment in buses, the government is pressing ahead with privatising British Rail. On current projections, investment in Britain's rail infrastructure until the end of the century will be lower in per route mile terms than any other European country except Norway and Sweden (Steer Davies Gleave, 1994). Unless a major effort is made to improve the quality of public transport and provide a package of complementary supportive measures, private motorists are not going to switch from private to public transport in the short term. There is little current evidence that the necessary investment in either public transport – given continuing privatisation – or traffic calming schemes will be forthcoming.

The prospect of new commercial investment being channelled into existing centres is welcome. But many authorities fear that car restraint will play into the hands of existing out-of-centre locations unless quality alternative modes of transport are offered. Limiting car parking provision in town centres could deter car-borne shoppers and damage retailing and commercial interests. Retailers may have even more reason to move out-of-town. More employers may also relocate or encourage additional home working. As a result, local authorities might attempt to secure economic development at any price even on peripheral sites not well served by public transport. If excessive numbers of cars are allowed to clog core areas, this could trigger congestion and further decentralisation. It is hardly surprising that the government is reconsidering the introduction of road pricing in urban areas which could be misconstrued as a tax on car owners and businesses. Road pricing on radial routes into town centres needs to be explicitly linked to investment in public transport with incentives to companies to alter their practices, and rooted in a good understanding of local travel and traffic patterns and preferences.

The ultimate irony is that the government which deregulated public transport and liberalised planning policy in the 1980s, encouraging massive private sector investment in edge-of-town retail, service and leisure developments and the build up of developers' peripheral land banks, is now championing town centres and car restraint. It would have been difficult to create a more unpromising context in which to introduce their new planning guidance!

From an environmental perspective, however, the outlook is not entirely gloomy. In the longer term, the EU is introducing stricter emission controls. The technological means for eliminating virtually all smoke and particulates from diesel cars now exists. Most exhaust emissions from petrol cars will be progressively reduced since catalytic converters became obligatory on all new models in 1993. Car manufacturers are developing twin powered cars which can switch from running on petrol or diesel to being powered by electricity in built up areas. Furthermore, the insistence by certain US states that a proportion of new vehicles manufactured after 1996 are completely emission-free should bring down the production costs of alternatively powered vehicles which have been quite high. Environmentalists argue that the net effect on emission levels will be nil if the electricity for the cars is produced from fossil fuels, but even so the emissions would be spread over a wider area and hence air quality in congested locations such as town centres should dramatically improve. For the immediate future the main problems will remain $CO_2$ emissions and a steady growth in traffic partially offsetting the benefits from cleaner technology.

## Conclusion

Incalculable damage has been done to the fabric of Britain's town centres over the last two decades by the failure to balance public and private transport, the neglect of integrated land use and transport planning and chronic underinvestment in infrastructure. The car has become urban society's master rather than its servant. It has subjugated other forms of transport and inhibited the development of cities' social activities and networks. Cities were designed for people rather than cars. While the automobile initially opened up exchange opportunities by improving accessibility, those opportunities are now being destroyed by its dominance. If town centres are to remain both commercially viable and attractive places to be, much greater attention must be given to their capacity to handle vehicular traffic and preference given to environmentally friendly modes of transport. The key test will be whether traffic can be controlled so that people no longer reject living in town centres because of the congestion and pollution. Past policy failures do not augur well. But at least many now agree on the nature and severity of the challenge if not on the precise methods to deal with it.

## References

Appleyard, D. (1981) *Liveable Streets*, University of California, Berkeley.

Association of County Councils (1994) *Towards a Sustainable Transport Policy*, 2nd edition, ACC, London.

Benwell, M. (1994) 'Can transport be a private matter?', *The Chartered Institute of Transport, Proceedings*, 3 (3 ).

Buchanan, M. (1988) 'Urban transport and market forces in Britain', in Hass-Klau C. (ed.) *New Life for City Centres. Planning, Transport and Conservation in British and German Cities*, Anglo-German Foundation, London.

Civic Trust (1991) *Mortgage Express Civic Trust: Audit of the Environment*, Civic Trust, London.

Commission of the European Communities (1992) 'The impact of transport on the environment', Com (92) 46, Brussels.

Confederation of British Industry (1989) *Transport in London: the Capital at Risk*, CBI, London.

Department of Environment and Department of Transport (1993) 'Reducing transport emissions through planning', ECOTEC/Transportation Planning Associates, HMSO, London.

Department of Environment and Department of Transport (1994) 'Planning and transport', Planning Policy Guidance Note No.13, HMSO, London.

Department of Transport (1989) 'Road traffic forecasts', DoT, London.

Department of Transport (1990) ' "Traffic quotes". Public perceptions of traffic regulation in urban areas'. Report of a research study, Dr P. Jones, Transport Studies Unit, University of Oxford for Traffic Advisory Unit.

Hallett, S. (1990) 'Drivers attitudes towards driving, cars and traffic', Transport Studies Unit, Oxford University, Oxford.

Hillman, M. (1993) 'Cycling and the promotion of health', *Policy Studies*, 14 (2), pp. 49–59.

Holman, C. (1992) *Cleaner Buses: Ways of Reducing Pollution from Urban Buses*, Friends of the Earth, London.

Howard, D.F. (1991a) 'Public transport: the options', *The Planner*, TCPSS proceedings, 13 December.

Howard, D.F., Gentile, P. and Peterson, B.P. (1991b) 'Accessible cities for the twenty-first century', International Commission on Traffic and Urban Planning 49th International Congress, International Union of Public Transport, Brussels.

Jones, P. (1991) 'Public attitudes to options for dealing with traffic congestion in urban areas – what the pollsters say', Institute of British Geographers Annual Conference, Sheffield, 2–5 January.

Kenworthy, J. and Newman, P. (1989) *Cities and Automobile Dependence*, Gower Technical, Aldershot.

Laconte, P. (1992) 'Transportation networks in urban Europe', *Ekistics*, 352/353 pp. 93-113.

London Research Centre (1992) 'Paris London: a comparison of transport systems', Joint Study with l'Institut d'Amenagement et d'Urbanisme de la Région d'Île-de-France.

Morgan, J.M. (1991) 'Cycling in safety?', Transport and Road Research Laboratory, Crowthorne.

NEDO (1988) 'The future of the High Street', Distributive Trades Economic Development Committee, National Economic Development Office, HMSO, London.

Pharoah, T. (1992) *Less Traffic, Better Towns*, Friends of the Earth, London.

Royal Commission on Transport and Environmental Pollution (1994) *Transport and the Environment*, 18th report. Cm 2674, HMSO, London.

Sawyer, M. (1994) 'Driving the men wild', *Guardian*, 18 May.

Society of Motor Manufacturers and Traders (1994) 'Survey of buses and coaches', cited in *Guardian*, 28 September.

Standing Advisory Committee on Trunk Road Assessment (1993) 'Trunk roads and the generation of traffic', HMSO, London.

Steer Davies Gleave (1992) 'Financing public transport: how does Britain compare?'. Report to the Bow Group, the Centre for Local Economic Strategies, Eurotunnel, Railway Industries Association and Transport 2000.

Steer Davies Gleave (1994) 'Promoting rail investment', for Transport 2000, London.

Tolley, R. (ed.) (1990) *The Greening of Urban Transport*, Bellhaven Press, London.

Transport 2000 (1994) 'Myths and facts: transport trends and transport policies', Transport 2000, London.

UK Quality of Urban Air Review Group (1992) 'Urban air quality in the United Kingdom', First Report, HMSO, London.

Which (1990) 'Traffic in cities', *Which*, October.

World Wildlife Fund (1990) 'Public attitudes towards transport and pollution', WWF, Godalming.

# Chapter 4
# Offices – from boom to bust?

## Introduction

Nearly half of British employees work in offices. Town centres contain the largest concentrations of office employment because building societies, banks, legal, accountancy and insurance firms are based there. Public, personal and distributional services are also important sources of employment. However, the traditional advantages of a town centre location – access to a large pool of both labour and customers, contact with other firms and the availability of facilities for office employees – have been offset by the lack of room for expansion, traffic congestion, parking problems and costly overheads. Rapid development in transport and telecommunications technologies, together with a more permissive planning regime in the 1980s, have opened up a wider range of locations to service firms and enabled new forms of corporate organisation and work regime, such as teleworking and desk-sharing, to emerge. Cuts in public administration, restructuring and 'downsizing' within the financial services sector because of the recession and the introduction of labour saving technology have also raised questions about the viability of town centres as office locations. Their commercial dominance may be at risk. Despite these concerns, recent debate has focused upon retailing and transportation issues and ways of introducing a wider mix of land uses. Town centres' relative attractiveness as office locations and the changing characteristics and needs of town centre businesses have often been overlooked. Similarly, there is little research on office employment trends and dynamics and the relationship between offices, shopping and transport.

This chapter attempts to redress this imbalance. It begins with a discussion of recent developments in town centre office activity and the dynamics of change. The following section speculates upon town centres' future prospects as office locations. The chapter concludes by discussing the policy implications of both recent and projected patterns of commercial development in the town centres.

## Trends and dynamics in town centre office activity

### *A twentieth-century growth phenomenon*

The scale of office activity has varied enormously in different town centres for a number of reasons: the size of the catchment population, the town's administrative status, the importance of indigenous service firms, location, attractiveness to inward investment and the nature and strength of the sub-regional economy. However, most have grown in commercial importance for a large part of the present century. This has stemmed mainly from the sustained expansion of producer services such as banking, insurance and finance, post and telecommunications, public services, administration and research and development. In the period 1920–91, producer services' share of total town centre employment grew rapidly from 3 per cent to 15 per cent while public services and administration increased from 9 per cent to 27 per cent. By contrast, distributive services, including retailing, grew only slowly from 19.3 per cent to 19.5 per cent of total employment. Personal services, such as hotels and catering, and recreational and cultural activities diminished in significance from 13 per cent to 10 per cent (Simmie *et al.*, 1993). As accountancy, insurance, financial, property management and distributional services to manufacturers became more specialised, sophisticated and interrelated after the First World War, the advantages of locating together within central business districts outweighed those associated with being based at points of production. Town centres have also benefited from the long-term growth in the average size of operating unit within both public and private sectors motivated by economies of scale. Many such strategic, administrative and executive functions have located in core locations where they are most accessible to a substantial population.

Demands for central accommodation were initially met in the 1920s and 1930s by the construction of bespoke premises or the erection of combined shops and offices on a speculative basis, targeted mainly at retailers. However, growing shortages of space soon resulted in redevelopment at greater density and height and also physical expansion of the core. In many larger town centres, tall office blocks were built in the late 1950s. During that time an unprecedented boom in office construction began and continued well into the 1970s. Economic recovery, along with the credit squeeze, brought together development companies and liquid insurance companies which undertook large-scale office development on a speculative basis for the first time. The freezing of commercial rents in London in 1964 followed by the introduction of government controls upon office development and encouraging office firms to relocate elsewhere meant that the boom rapidly spread to provincial town and city centres. Burgeoning bank lending and institutional investment further fuelled growth. Local authorities zoned areas for new office complexes, which led to the displacement of lower value uses such as housing and manufacturing firms. However, rising interest rates combined with falling demand led to a property crash in 1974 and optimism gave way to uncertainty. Decline in manufacturing had a knock-on effect on the service sector and employment in public administration had to be cut back as part of the effort to redress the growing national trade deficit. Concern about the implications of new technology for jobs and space requirements also suppressed development interest as did a decentralisation of population and jobs to the suburbs and smaller towns in surrounding sub-regions. During the early 1980's recession the amount of office development in most town centres diminished to a trickle.

### *Recent trends in office development – winners and losers*

Over the last ten years, patterns of office development and trends in office employment have become more uneven. This is partly a reflection of divergent regional economic prospects and the decentralisation of population and economic activity. The perceptions and behaviour of the property development industry, financiers and the decisions of externally based multi-national conglomerates have been crucial, too. The uneven impact of the unparalleled boom in office construction in the late 1980s demonstrates this clearly. Supply of office space in 1990 was double the level achieved at the previous peak of the property cycle in 1973 (Nabarro and Key, 1992). This surge of activity stemmed from impressive growth in output and employment in the financial and business services sector. Financial deregulation, developments in information technology such as the widespread introduction of personal computers, the tendency of large corporations to contract out more work to reduce overheads led to a dramatic expansion of banking, financial services, accountancy and legal services. The emergence of novel business service activities such as advertising and marketing, graphic design, computer services and management consultancy further boosted employment. Equally important, such expansion altered accommodation requirements and rendered much existing stock obsolete. More flexible, expansive layouts, raised floors and suspended ceilings and ducting for computer cables and other services were increasingly in demand.

The development industry responded enthusiastically to such demands since dramatic increases in bank lending helped to compensate for only modest institutional investment at the time. However, this boom in activity principally benefited Central London and London Docklands and town centres in the south east, especially those in growth corridors like Reading and Bracknell on the M4. But provincial town centres benefited only to a modest extent. Developers and institutions were both inclined to invest on the basis of historic rental growth performance, hence the south eastern bias. As a result, recent patterns of office development and investment have reinforced the past structural characteristics of local and sub-regional economies and failed to meet emerging indigenous needs. The pursuit of past success, as opposed to detailed market analysis, has been a major factor holding back development in less buoyant areas. Reports that occupants have stripped out overspecified and overpriced offices suggest that developers may have overreacted to one particular demand segment and not supplied what the market required in growth areas either.

*The emergence of competing office locations*

The late 1980s also witnessed the emergence for the first time of significant concentrations of office development in out-of-town locations The volume of new office development in out-of-town business parks grew in the period 1985–92 from negligible proportions to equal that of town centre office construction as a whole. Their superior performance in terms of investment return compared to other types of offices in the period 1985–91 is testament both to their popularity and the threat they pose to town centres (Scott and Parry, 1992). However, the incidence of business parks has been patchy. The great majority are located in the south east, on the edges of major provincial cities or other relatively prosperous areas, typically near to airports and national road networks. The degree of exposure of town centres to competition from new office locations has varied considerably.

**Table 4.1: Strengths and weaknesses of competing office locations**

| | Town centre | Out-of-town centre |
|---|---|---|
| Positive | Public transport node | Accessibility |
| | Shopping and recreational facilities | Pleasant environment |
| | Arts and cultural facilities | Image |
| | Proximity to related firms | Proximity to homes |
| | | Car parking |
| | | Cost savings |
| | | More space |
| Negative | Increased congestion, shortage of car parking | Lacking range of shopping, arts and catering facilities |
| | Increased accommodation costs | Variable public transport service |
| | Longer commuting times | |
| | Lack of space | |
| | Pollution, crime, degraded environment | |

*Source*: based on Debenham Tewson Research, 1990.

Table 4.1 identifies why out-of-centre locations have been able to compete successfully with traditional locations. A number of push and pull factors stand out. The principal push factors have been the cost and growing inaccessibility of core areas because of growing car dependency, limited car parking, congestion and a lack of response to office firms' changing accommodation needs. Others have argued that decentralisation has been inevitable because strict control of building heights has exacerbated problems of lack of space and excessively high property values, unlike cities in the United States and the Far East where high-rise office development has maintained a closer balance between supply and demand (Schiller, 1988).

There have, nevertheless, been strong positive reasons for decentralisation. Advances in telecommunications have enabled large banking and insurance companies to relocate 'back office' functions such as clerical and data-processing jobs to cheaper, more extensive out-of-centre offices with ample car parking. They have retained smaller executive offices and customer facilities involving frequent personal communication within town centres. Some firms have opted for out-of-town locations because their customer base has become more decentralised and dispersed, and because of growing space demands, the lure of superior out-of-town environments and the opportunity to exchange outmoded central premises for buildings which have their own unique identity. Developers prefer out-of-town locations because they are easier places in which to develop modern offices. These buildings usually have an extensive uninterrupted floor area which can be fitted out to firms' own specifications and easily adapted to suit changing space requirements. Land and premises can more readily be released in response to shifts in demand than in town centres where land acquisition problems and objections from neighbouring interests and amenity groups often result in greater lead times and market oversupply.

The Conservative government's earlier easing of planning restrictions paved the way for extensive development outside town centres in the late 1980s. New government circulars advised local planning authorities not to seek to influence the volume and location of office development and economic activity by appraising whether development was needed and using office floorspace controls. Local authorities were requested to focus mainly upon physical land use issues (DoE, 1985). This, together with a general exhortation that local authorities should favour development, accelerated decentralisation of office activity and generated additional office development in other parts of the built-up area. However, the out-of-town business park phenomenon stemmed directly from amendments to planning legislation. Revision of the Use Classes Order (UCO) in 1987 and General Development Order (GDO) in 1988 meant that changes of use within a new business class known as the B1 category incorporating office, research and development and light industrial uses no longer required planning permission (DoE, 1987, 1988). Earlier out-of-town developments had been designed for high-tech, research and development companies seeking a clean production environment. But developers could now take advantage of the B1 category in the 1987 UCO and offer business space to a wide range of office firms seeking high quality, flexible accommodation in a low density, spacious, attractively landscaped setting. The 1 million square foot development at Stockley Park, near Heathrow was a notable example of the new breed. Premises originally intended for high tech industry and research and development companies could now be marketed for offices. Buildings with permission for general industrial uses could also now be converted to offices without the need for planning permission.

Such revisions to the UCO and GDO also enabled firms to relocate from town centres to other parts of urban areas even more easily. In London, for example, growing demand for smaller, preferably freehold, office suites in cheaper locations prompted the conversion of inns and public houses to financial and professional services uses without the need to obtain planning permission. There is also evidence that traditional manufacturing areas such as Saville Row and Hatton Garden have been partially transformed into unplanned office areas because of the financial advantages to landowners (London Boroughs Association, 1992). There have also been reports of landowners seeking to convert light industrial and warehousing space to offices in areas on the fringe of town centres following the creation of the B1 category.

The collapse of the property market in 1990 and the subsequent deep recession led to a rapid contraction in the number of business services jobs and also slowed decentralisation, especially in the south east (Jones Lang and Wootton, 1994). An extreme example was Central London, where almost as many service sector jobs were lost in the three years 1989–92 as had been created in the previous six. The oversupply of office space there meant that the gap between rentals in central and peripheral locations narrowed sharply, and the comparative advantage of locating out-of-town diminished. Many firms simply became too preoccupied with survival to contemplate a move. Other tenants had no choice but to remain *in situ* because the recession made it difficult for them to reassign institutional leases.

### *Changes in the nature and location of town centre offices*

There have been more modest but significant developments within town centre office quarters in the last decade. Demand for more modern flexible, extensive floorspace resulted in a limited amount of commercial development in many town and city centres, especially the larger ones and those located in more prosperous locations. However, development also occurred sporadically in less buoyant town centres where there was public support such as City Grant or English Estates finance. Some locations gained at the expense of others because they were more able to accommodate the latest offices. These were bulkier, if squatter, in construction and contained uninterrupted floorspace and raised floors, lowered ceilings and ducting for modern servicing requirements.

There have been notable shifts of activity within the existing stock. The most noticeable development trend has been the polarisation of most town centre office markets. On the one hand, there is a continuing healthy demand for modern or recently refurbished offices in core locations, as many tenants seek prominent positions. Funding institutions prefer to invest in prime town centre properties capable of attracting prestigious and financially secure tenants and generating a good return over the long term. On the other hand, there is a secondary market of property which is increasingly difficult to let. Either it is unsuited to modern requirements, has the wrong image or is in a poor position – over a shop or in a run-down fringe location. Such space is increasingly likely to be demolished or converted to other uses. The reasons for this growing divide are not fully understood. The increase in volume of vacant secondary space may be due to demand deficiency. This has many causes including loss of activity to other locations, relocation to more modern central premises, abandonment of office space over shops as a result of concentration or contracting out support functions or finally, rationalisation and restructuring both within the public administration and the financial services sector. But supply can be a problem. Property owners are sometimes reluctant to modernise accommodation because of market uncertainty and lack of investment in the vicinity. Owners often have unrealistic expectations of their property's worth because prices are artificially inflated by a few deals. They also tend to retain property in its current use because of its potential investment value and concern that short-term non-commercial usage of the building might detract from its long-term value. Alternatively, polarisation in the property market may reflect the distinction between a core of secure prestigious service companies and a more peripheral group of less secure firms whose livelihood depends upon short-term contracts. The precise explanation varies in different towns. What is certain is that major structural change is underway. Dramatic restructuring in the banking and finance sector during the current recession gives some idea of the scale of the transition.

Throughout the 1980s, expansion in the number of outlets occupied by estate agents, banks, building societies and insurance companies helped to compensate for the decline of secondary retail areas due to the growth of out-of-town retailing, the reduced number but increasing size of shops and concentration of the most prestigious stores within prime areas. However, the depth and duration of the recession and depressed consumer expenditure have forced financial services companies to improve operational efficiency and reduce overheads by substituting new technology for labour, concentrating the majority of their activities at cheaper locations and retaining only sales operations in prime locations. Banks and building societies, for example, have rationalised networks and abandoned comprehensive service provision in favour of 'hub and spoke operations' where limited local facilities are backed by a full range of services at main offices.

Such restructuring has had four main implications for town centres (Richardson, 1994). First, employment in financial services sectors has fallen reducing patronage of nearby shops. Increased use of automatic teller machines in banks and building societies, use of credit cards and electronic transfer of funds, closure or scaling down of activities in smaller branches, and custom lost because of competition from cheaper telephone banking have all led to job losses. Rationalisation has particularly affected smaller town centres because minor branches have been most vulnerable to closure or downgrading either to self-service facilities or outlets offering only basic services. Second, organisational restructuring and greater use of technology has altered the accommodation needs of banks and building societies. Banks are not only minimising their overall number of outlets but also closing down street-corner branches and acquiring smaller units with large glass frontages in areas of maximum pedestrian activity where the emphasis is upon selling financial products to the public. Traditional banking functions are increasingly handled automatically and enquiry and data processing functions are being grouped together in cheaper out-of-centre locations. Third, rationalisation has re-emphasised the process of spatial retrenchment within town centre property markets. Financial and other producer services are no longer compensating for the decline in retailing in secondary shopping areas as they did in the late 1980s. Indeed, their preference for prime space is hastening the demise of secondary areas. Fourth, restructuring is changing the physical character and feel of town centres. Although town centres in theory offer limitless possibilities for social activity, many transactions are becoming more and more impersonal. The move away from personal cashier service to cash machines may be convenient to the customer in a narrow sense but if taken to extremes the overall effect will be to further reduce social contact. Moreover, the new financial service outlets lack the character of traditional street corner premises and have a deadening effect upon prime retail areas. More imaginative frontage design and displays are required if they are to add to, rather than detract from, the vitality and variety of the High Street.

Such transformations raise more fundamental questions about whether town centre businesses have wider responsibilities in terms of customer care and personal attention and promoting social activity within town centres. The 1980s office tower clad in reflective glass is a suitable symbol of current commercial values – parasitic, inward looking and lacking in distinctiveness and intrinsic merit. Such enterprises have profited greatly from their prime position but contributed little to the quality of life and environmental attractiveness of individual town centres.

### Prospects for town centres offices

There are sharply differing views about the future of town centre commercial districts. Doom-mongers predict mass abandonment. As office quarters become expensive and inefficient and the amount of teleworking increases, hiring of premises in a variety of employment locations for short-term contractual work becomes a more attractive option. Optimists, on the other hand, believe that the conversion of offices to a wider range of uses will herald a new dawn for town centres. They predict that town centres will become more diverse, appealing and lively places where people will want to spend leisure time and live as well as work. Whichever prediction proves the more accurate, major change is in the offing.

The future scale and location of office activity will depend upon: the interplay between economic and employment prospects;

changes in locational and space requirements; the behaviour of the property development industry; and public policy. The overall prospects for office employment appear reasonably healthy. Most economic forecasts agree that the number of employees in office-based occupations will increase. The Institute for Employment Research (IER) has predicted that in the period 1988–2000, the number of such jobs will increase from 12.4 million to over 14 million (IER, 1992). However, most growth is expected in managerial and professional occupations. Numbers of secretarial and clerical staff are expected to change only slightly and may decrease as a result of increasing use of information technology. This is mixed news for town centres. The total number of jobs will probably fall since the major proportion of their employees are clerical white collar workers. More positively, their continuing attractiveness to service activities requiring personal contact and executive decision making will partially offset such employment losses.

However, town centres will be vulnerable to continued waves of rationalisation and restructuring within existing firms. The constant search for ways to minimise overheads means that executives will increasingly question the wisdom of tying up costs in large town centre premises. Large, mono-functional office buildings are an expensive luxury because they incur high overheads and are underutilised. In a typical calendar year, an office block is utilised only for about 20 per cent of the time. Its central position also generates other costs such as those associated with commuting. Banks and building societies will continue to cut overheads and rationalise their space requirements and increasingly switch to tele-sales and tele-banking operations. Further advances in telematics will enable service sector employees to adopt more flexible working patterns by plugging in to central computer systems from home, clients' premises, transport vehicles, hotels and leisure facilities. This will have three effects. First, firms in all locations will experiment with alternative working practices such as the continued application of new technology, desk sharing and a greater amount of teleworking. This will reduce their space demands and overheads and hence boost productivity (Hillman, 1993). Second, office firms will be more inclined to demand flexible space on flexible terms to minimise unnecessary overheads and accommodate shifting space needs. Proportionately more space will be needed for meetings rather than desk space, for example. During the current recession, landlords have been forced to offer shorter leases to secure lettings. In future, the institutional lease is less likely to offer town centres a form of insulation from short-term changes in market conditions. Third, more dispersed working patterns coupled with demands from manufacturing clients for frequent personal contact with contractors will result in the decentralisation of further functions to out-of-town locations and the paring back of town centre staff. In the 1980s, high tech, service distribution, financial services, insurance and media companies were more inclined to decentralise their operations than professional services companies such as accountants and lawyers. Now even the latter are contemplating moving their routine operations to locations such as business parks because of the cost savings (DTZ Debenham Thorpe, 1993). These trends suggest that substantial amounts of downtown office accommodation will become surplus to requirements.

Despite this, there is scope for town centre interests to limit decentralisation by building upon their inherent advantages and sharpening their competitive edge. Service companies still value town centres' traditional advantages such as ability to service large catchment areas, access to a sizeable pool of labour and sophistication of related services. Also, new forms of working practices have their limitations. Teleworking has its critics. Many are concerned about loneliness and lack of social contact, family tensions, lack of personal motivation and managerial oversight and inferior terms and conditions of employment. Also, much business still involves personal contact. This suggests that firms will continue to locate key decision-making and some customer service functions in town centres with more routine operations out-of-town.

Town centres' appeal will depend heavily upon local authorities and central government's level of investment in infrastructure and their policy stance both towards admissible types of business in prime areas and development in competing locations. The increased popularity of town centre management signifies an end to past complacency and a fresh determination to counter competition from out-of-town centres. But further traffic congestion could hasten the departure of office firms. It is also difficult to see how town centres are going to maintain their comparative advantage in providing cultural and leisure attractions given a lack of resources for extensive clearance and redevelopment or refurbishment of redundant office buildings and related infrastructure. Developers of out-of town business parks will narrow the gap by providing an increasingly sophisticated range of staff facilities such as restaurants, pubs, leisure uses, nurseries and crèches. In addition, out-of-town retail locations will continue to attract a wider range of support services such as post offices and banks which were once found mainly in the High Street. If the next round of mega-business park proposals materialises with improvements in the economy, future planning policies will be decisive. Also a continuation of present policies on change of use is bound to result in further conversion of light industrial and warehousing space elsewhere in built-up areas into offices, further sapping town centres' commercial strength.

Although the extreme scenarios seem poles apart, they share a common premise. This is that growing concerns about sustainability, quality of life and the costs of growth in travel demand mean that the travel distance between home and work will in future diminish. The degree to which town centres maintain and develop a distinctive cultural and leisure appeal and become more popular places to live will crucially influence their ability to compete successfully with out-of-town locations. Town centres seem set to maintain their traditional advantage over business parks in providing lunchtime and after-work shopping opportunities. Significant retail provision has not proved viable in out-of-centre business locations. There is also growing interest in the feasibility of converting redundant and unmarketable office space to residential and other uses. The success of the 'Living over the Shop' (LOTS) initiative, described in further detail in Chapter 7, has prompted some private property owners to convert redundant offices to housing. However, the extent of such repopulating is modest, mainly limited to London and a handful of major provincial cities. The future scale of conversion is likely to be constrained for a variety of financial, institutional, planning and technical reasons unless action is taken by government and other town centre interests. The principal problems include: the unrealistic attitude of property owners hoping for an upturn in the market; VAT charges on refurbishment; grant eligibility; Local Planning Authorities' fears about further loss of employment space and unrealistic density and car parking standards; and technical problems associated with, for example, high floor to ceiling heights, inadequate access and the cost of satisfying fire regulations (Barlow and Gann, 1993). Such accommodation appeals mainly to young professionals, students and those needing social housing. There are few signs that the quality of the inner urban environment, schooling and leisure facilities will be upgraded sufficiently to persuade families or older people to move back into town centres in numbers. Attempts to locate employment and residential uses closer together, along with more dispersed working practices, will favour out-of-town office locations.

In the longer term the government's emphasis upon sustainability and minimising travel demand could also affect the internal distribution of office activity within town centres. Office locations which are near to major transport termini will be regarded more favourably by both developers and users than those which are solely accessible by car. This could either reinforce or modify the recent tendency for spatial polarisation of core office markets depending upon the position of bus and rail stations and routes. The most likely scenario is that office activity will slowly continue to drift out-of-town. Town centre interests will have to struggle much harder to retain, let alone attract, office firms in future. The main challenges will be to raise sufficient resources to improve accessibility and make use of the increasing amount of redundant space for social, recreational and residential purposes. A richer mix of land uses could make town centre environments more lively, sustainable and attractive places than in the past. There is also scope to experiment with new forms of accommodation such as letting space on flexible terms and offering rented homes-cum-offices for short-term contract workers and around-the-clock use of space for multiple purposes. Equally, local authorities and other town centre interests may be able to compensate for higher overheads and underutilisation by investing heavily in energy-efficiency schemes such as installation of computer-controlled heating, ventilation and lighting systems.

## Conclusion

In future, town centre planners, developers and property owners will have to devote much closer attention to the changing accommodation requirements and other needs of firms and perhaps show a more flexible attitude to accommodating business uses such as solicitors in prime areas. Improving the quality of life of their workers will also be of paramount importance. Much office development has lacked distinctive character. Rather more attention has been paid to the quality of the internal working environment and providing car access rather than on-site leisure facilities. The way in which such buildings relate to neighbouring land uses, transportation nodes and the broader street scene has been overlooked. From the late 1950s a substantial proportion of office development has been constructed on a speculative nature with little regard for enhancing the overall quality of life of office workers or upgrading the broader town centre environment. But the age of unimaginative single use office buildings within mono-functional commercial areas which are dead and abandoned outside normal working hours is over. In future, it will be a case of adapt or die. Developments like Broadgate in London, where office development is interwoven with amenity space, street sculpture, arts and leisure activities and linked effectively with public transportation systems, must become more commonplace if town centres are going to stem the flight of commerce.

Stemming the decline will be crucial on equity grounds. Office activities provide a valuable source of employment for inner city residents, especially the relatively unskilled. The loss of junior and clerical staff in the banking sector following the introduction of new technology has already exerted a heavy toll. Decentralisation of employment and further rationalisation would lead to further heavy job losses in cleaning, packaging, secretarial and clerical occupations heightening poverty in deprived areas. The retention of a slimmed down corps of managers could be socially unsustainable in such circumstances since they would become the focus of resentment and vulnerable to crime and personal attack. That would probably lead either to the construction of fortified office complexes of the type found in inner Los Angeles or mass abandonment of town centres. Both would be an admission of failure.

## References

Barlow, J. and Gann, D. (1993) *Offices into Flats*, Joseph Rowntree Foundation, York.

Debenham Tewson Research (1990) 'Business parks – out of town or out of touch?', Debenham Tewson and Chinnocks, London.

Department of Environment (1985) 'Development and employment', Circular 14/85, HMSO, London.

Department of Environment (1987) 'The Town and Country Planning (Use Classes) Order 1987', Statutory Instrument No.

764, HMSO, London.

Department of Environment (1988) 'Amendments to the Town and Country Planning General Development Order', HMSO, London.

DTZ Debenham Thorpe (1993) 'Business parks: prospects for the 1990s', special report, DTZ Debenham Thorpe, London.

Healey, P., Davoudi S., O'Toole M., Tavsanoglu S. and Usher D. (eds) (1992). *Rebuilding the City. Property-led Urban Regeneration*, E. & F.N. Spon, London.

Hillman, J. (1993) *Tele-lifestyles and the Flexicity: a European Study – the Impact of the Electronic Home*, OOPEC, Luxembourg.

Institute for Employment Research (1992) 'Review of the economy and employment', IER, Warwick.

Jones Lang and Wootton (1994) 'The decentralisation of offices from central London – an annual special survey', Jones Lang and Wootton, London.

London Boroughs Association (1992) 'Out of order! The 1987 Use Classes Order: problems and proposals', LBA, London.

Nabarro, R. and Key, T. (1992) 'Current trends in commercial property investment and development: an overview', in Healey P., Davoudi S., O'Toole M., Tavsanoglu S. and Usher D. (eds) (1992).

Richardson, R. (1994) 'Finance floods out of thc High Street', *Planning Week*, 2 (13), pp. 10–11.

Schiller, R. (1988) 'Office decentralisation lessons from America', *Estates Gazette*, 4, pp. 20–2.

Scott, I. and Parry, M. (1992) 'The makings of a star performer', *Estates Gazette*, 9224, pp. 25–6.

Simmie, J., Penn, A. and Sutcliffe, A. (1993) 'The death and life of town centres', Bartlett School of Planning, University College, London.

# Chapter 5
# The deterioration of the public realm

## Introduction

Town centres perform a vital social function because they contain important public spaces, arts and cultural venues and meeting places. However, a set of powerful economic, political, institutional and social forces threaten to undermine their wider social purpose. Investors, property owners and shoppers see town centres primarily as places of investment, profit or consumption. Local authorities have regarded the commercial functions of town centres and their transportation infrastructure as crucial but have neglected other social aspects. Many out-of-town retail and business parks now possess more modern, convenient and accessible retail stores and office accommodation, leisure facilities and well managed environments, but they lack the sense of place and atmosphere of longer-established town centres. Town centre interests will in future need to reconcile the enhancement of their historic character and cultural assets with development of their economic infrastructure and transportation systems.

This chapter analyses the extent to which this balance has been achieved. The first section investigates town centres' social significance using the concept of 'the public realm'. The next section examines the shifting nature and status of the public realm within town centres and the underlying dynamics of change. The concluding section speculates on the likely outcome of the interplay between town centres' commercial and social roles in future. Throughout, it draws upon the growing literature on the subject of the public realm (e.g. Bianchini, 1990; Montgomery, 1990; Worpole, 1992; Biddulph, 1993).

## The social significance of town centres

There are clear, quantifiable indicators of the commercial success of town centres but assessing their social significance is a more subjective affair. Residents and visitors relate to particular town centres in different ways. A combination of good attractions, ease of accessibility and attractive and safe public spaces are critical to their popularity (DoE, 1994). However, town centres' more elusive qualities, such as intrinsic character, symbolism, historical significance and atmosphere, affect patronage too because these qualities can engender feelings ranging from a sense of belonging to complete alienation. How and why town centres acquire social meaning is under-researched. With some exceptions (e.g. Comedia, 1991; Civic Trust, 1993), little research has been conducted on popular perceptions of the quality of town centre environments. Most 'quality of life' studies are pitched at the urban level, or investigate levels of material prosperity rather than views upon the quality of the urban experience. More generally, there has been a persistent failure to apply the scientific findings of research in environmental psychology to urban design and planning (Beer, 1991).

### *Town centres and the public realm*

It is possible to outline different conceptions of town centres' social role and potential and test the underlying assumptions. Some commentators have argued that town centres are significant in social terms because they are a key component of the public realm (Comedia, 1991; Worpole, 1992). Bianchini defined the public realm as 'that realm of social relations going beyond one's own circle of family, professional and social relations' (Bianchini, 1990). This drew upon Lofland's distinction between the primary realm of household and personal networks, the parochial realm of community networks and the public realm which comprises public spaces or places where strangers are most likely to be encountered (Lofland, 1989). Although the concept of the public realm has no precise spatial or physical parallels, town centres present rich possibilities for such relations since they are shared public spaces which lie beyond particular residential neighbourhoods. They contain many indoor meeting places such as theatres, museums, cinemas and art galleries and are the scene of street entertainment and public events. Town centres present a variety of opportunites for the chance encounter, exchange of personal views and experiences, confrontation of prejudices and challenges to received wisdom, and also street protests and demonstrations. They provide an alternative set of experiences to the more familiar sequence of events within the home or workplace. Town centres are barometers of public social life since they constitute neutral territory, represent cosmopolitan values and the focus of civic identity (Comedia, 1991). Since they are frequently points of arrival for newcomers or those returning home and often contain key public spaces, they often shape the urban experience.

### *Urban design and social behaviour*

The theories of behavioural psychologists and urban designers also suggest that town centres play an important role in shaping public social life. Lynch, identified the ways in which the physical qualities of public space interact with social processes to produce quality places (Lynch, 1984). He identified seven main contributory factors, which are presented in Table 5.1. Both urban practitioners and theorists have argued that different facets of urban design such as respect for context, sensitive choice of materials and scale and proportion can fundamentally affect social behaviour and the quality of the urban experience (Punter, 1990; Hayward and McGlynn, 1993).

### *Social protection and responsibility*

There are, however, alternative perspectives. Town centres may be barometers of standards of public social life. But their ability to influence individual and collective behaviour may not be as great as some assume. While they may in theory be the repository of the finest civic virtues, in practice they are particularly vulnerable to many of society's problems such as crime and anti-social activity. This more pessimistic view implies that town centres tend to mirror societal problems and national and institutional power relations and processes.

**Table 5.1: Ingredients of quality public spaces**

| | |
|---|---|
| *vitality* | public spaces whose form supports the health and biological functioning of the town's inhabitants |
| *sense of place* | spaces perceived as celebrating local culture and history, rich in symbolism and providing visual amenity and settings for celebration and display |
| *accesss* | paces offering universal accessibility |
| *fit* | paces which work well because they accommodate users' wishes and meet their needs |
| *control* | spaces which respect individuals' desire for privacy and ability to influence level of interaction |
| *justice* | spaces which balance enviromental gains among people |
| *efficiency* | spaces which balance different values |

*Source*: based on Lynch, 1984.

*Social needs*

There may be a mid-course between these two positions. Maslow, for example, has argued that quality of life increases as one progresses up a hierarchy of needs and wants beginning with the fulfilment of basic physiological requirements (air, food, water) and the need for security (shelter, safety), then social needs (group membership, belonging), and ultimately to satisfying the ego (self-image) and self-fulfilment (achievement of maximum potential) (Maslow, 1970). This line of thought implies that provision of a range of accessible basic retail and commercial services and a safe environment are an essential foundation if more individualist goals are to prove attainable. It also recognises that satisfaction of social and cultural needs by maximising scope for social interaction should precede achievement of more individualistic, personal goals, which involve purchase of strictly non-essential goods. While town centres may specialise in meeting 'higher order' needs, failure to provide simultaneously for social needs is ultimately self-defeating because it produces divisiveness and resentment. Hence, public safety and personal behaviour and responsibility and a well-designed and resourced public realm go hand in hand. Despite their varied emphasis, different theories therefore point to the importance of understanding and accommodating the social significance of town centres.

*Practical evidence of the importance of the social dimension*
Town centres contain a wide variety of facilities which are used and perceived in many different ways. They are arenas where production, consumption, enjoyment, tradition, self-identification, solidarity and social support jostle and overlap with one another. Retailing is a social phenomenon as well as a business activity. Cafes and restaurants are just as important as meeting places and social spaces as the more public open spaces. But the social well-being of town centres hinges most critically upon the condition, design and feel of shared, universally accessible public spaces which make up the public realm. In straightforward land use terms, the spaces between buildings such as streets, squares, and other public spaces can account for up to half the area of most town centres. The attractiveness of public spaces is determined by the quality of materials used, level of maintenance, lighting and landscaping which all significantly affect a town centre's popularity.

Popular public spaces share certain characteristics. Table 5.2 summarises these attributes. It suggests each conceptualisation of town centres' social significance has validity. Design, ease of access, developing local cultural identity and enhancing the public realm are important ingredients of popularity. New means of public protection such as the deployment of close circuit television cameras or urban rangers indicate that public safety considerations are increasingly important. Some public spaces are memorable and popular because they feature prominent landmarks, junctions, corridors and definite boundaries. These figure in mental maps which people construct to orientate themselves. Hence the strength of public opposition to the recent proposal to demolish the tall, cylindrical building in the otherwise reviled Bull Ring Shopping Centre, Birmingham, as it dominates, and adds interest to, an otherwise flat landscape. Mental imagery may also explain why the construction of gateways, such as the arched entrance to Chinatown, Manchester, have proved so effective in creating a sense of expectation and enclosure and have subsequently concentrated investment.

**Table 5.2: Attributes of popular public spaces within town centres**

| Attribute | Example |
|---|---|
| *Design* | |
| • Flexible, attractive space for varied street entertainment, public events | amphitheatre at Broadgate, Covent Garden |
| • Intricacy, detail, unusual character | The Lanes, Brighton; Shambles, York |
| • Opportunity for people-watching | hotel conservatories, Llandrinddod Wells |
| • Lively streetscene, network of cafes, meeting places and pedestrian routes | Nottingham |
| • Welcoming spaces, feeling of belonging and being under no obligation to justify presence | Basingstoke |
| • Spacious, well-designed surroundings balancing desire for privacy and company | Cardiff |
| • Investment of care and effort | Birmingham |
| • Use of natural assets | the river at St Albans |
| • Mix of activity, familiarity, novelty; neither fossilisation nor chaos | Chester |
| • Diversification of uses – e.g. pubs, libraries and churches | Whitehaven |
| • Comfortable sitting areas with good vistas | Harrogate |
| • Meeting places | town square, Horsham |
| • Vibrant night-time economy, cultural attractions | Newcastle; Nottingham; Leeds 24 Hour City initiative |
| *Safety* | |
| • Liveliness, lots of people of all ages, self-policing | Shrewsbury |
| • Avoidance of excessive landscaping to minimise threat of attack | |
| • Good lighting for pedestrians as well as motorists | |
| • Safe, comfortable, public space | Hammersmith |

| | |
|---|---|
| • Attention to special needs | |
| • Security with a humane face | mall ladies, Millgate Centre, Sheffield |
| • Absence of excessive litter, vandalism, temporary use of vacant shops, graffiti, vacant premises | Elephant and Castle |
| *Access* | |
| • Good pedestrian network | Nottingham |
| • Avoidance of clutter | Cheltenham |
| • Traffic calming, pro-pedestrian design | downgrading Birmingham Inner Ring Road |
| • Permeability and clear directions, maps, guides | bus station, Harrow |
| • Safe car parking | Sunderland; Exeter; Chichester |
| *Cultural identity* | |
| • Local distinctiveness, individuality | Chesterfield and Doncaster markets |
| • Historical continuity: preservation of treasured features, symbols, childhood memories | Exploring Living Memory Museum in Blackheath |
| • Good, free, arts attractions | Hounslow Centre Space; Croydon Library |
| • Celebration of indigenous culture(s) | Notting Hill Carnival |
| • Creation, enhancement of distinct quarters | Sheffield Cultural Quarter; Little Germany, Bradford; Birmingham Jewellery Quarter; Temple Bar, Dublin |
| • Catering for range of ages, tastes | tea dances for the elderly; non-alcoholic drinks in pubs |
| • Public art | Harrow |

*Source*: based on Comedia, 1991; Hubbard, 1993; DoE, 1994; Civic Trust, 1993.

Town centres need to blend four qualities if they are to be commercially and socially popular. They are:

- a critical mass of attractions;
- easy access and good pedestrian linkages;
- attractive streets and public spaces which are safe and possess a sense of local identity;
- the organisational and financial ability to make future improvements (DoE, 1994).

A recent retail study asked a sample of 2,500 shoppers in the county of Cheshire to list important factors in deciding where to shop (Herring Baker Harris and Intermarket Research, 1995). Price (51 per cent), car parking (42 per cent), easy car access (33 per cent), good range of shops (31 per cent) emerged as the most decisive reasons while more qualitative factors such as pleasant atmosphere (23 per cent), pedestrianised streets (16 per cent) somewhere to sit (10 per cent) and leisure facilities (4 per cent) were less important. This suggests that qualitative factors play a valuable supporting role but are no substitute in retailing terms for accessible shops which provide a range of decently-priced goods. However, this is not the whole story. The quality of the public realm would rate more highly if quality of life of office workers, the role of town centres in arts and tourism, and residential attractiveness were taken into account. Evidence from the Safer City Programme shows that public spaces which are seen as dangerous or as places to avoid reduce custom. Surveys in Islington and Manchester both revealed that women and older people are reluctant to visit these particular centres because they associate environmental degradation with criminal activity (Trench *et al.*, 1992). The character of the public realm has the potential to improve or undermine the commercial viability and the cultural appeal of town centres.

## Recent changes in the public realm

The public realm in many town and city centres has endured the urban equivalent of the 'tragedy of the commons'. Common usage of a collective environmental and social asset leads to over-exploitation, misuse and despoliation. Public spaces need careful, systematic public management but this has been lacking. 'Cities do not, any more than gardens, look after themselves' and this applies equally to town centres (Hillman, 1988). This section discusses the factors which have contributed to the deterioration in the public realm in town centres.

*Commercial dominance*
In the past few decades, the restructuring and modernisation of town centres has been dictated by powerful retail and commercial interests. Purpose-built environments were created in the 1960s and 1970s to improve access and servicing arrangements, and position premises to maximise pedestrian flows and turnover. The construction of covered shopping malls enabled better control of the retail environment such as protection from the elements, easier maintenance and cleansing, more scope for marketing and promotion. At the same time, however, such developments often erased traditional street blocks and effectively usurped public spaces for private ends. Many town centre thoroughfares are now artificial, stage-managed, environments under heavy surveillance during opening hours and dead zones at night – closed-off for security or management reasons. 'Undesirables' who might undermine the centre's image and popularity are often debarred from them. Since it is in landowners' and retailers' short-term interest to maximise floorspace and encourage circulation of pedestrians, social, cultural and recreational uses and even sitting areas have been neglected in such precincts.

Although most town centres have witnessed only incremental physical change since the mid-1970s, commercial exploitation of the public realm has continued. Property interests have increasingly latched on to the fascination with heritage by refurbishing run-down portions of real estate and marketing them as cultural quarters. In some cases, this has resulted in historical reinterpretation and the introduction of alien artefacts such as mass-produced period street furniture, 'olde worlde' facades and hence a confusing melange of the reproduced and the authentic. The public realm has been manipulated and even debased in the eyes of local people.

Many individual buildings have had a profound impact upon the streetscape. Public as well as private landowners, developers and other property interests have invested much greater attention in the image projected by individual buildings and their internal environment rather than ensuring that they blend with or complement their surroundings. More care has been invested, for example, in semi-private atria than in communal greenspace. While there is often no alternative to providing these internal green-spaces because of shortage of space, more could have been done to improve accessible neighbouring public spaces.

Retailers and other firms take advantage of the proximity of public space by advertising and using architectural symbolism to attract customers and project a conscious image. However, production of the built environment is increasingly controlled by a handful of externally based architects, designers, street furniture manufacturers and shopfitters. The same applies to shop interiors and the products on display, despite their increased range and sophistication. The standardisation of the street scene and shop interiors has affected the usage and enjoyment of neighbouring public spaces, however well-designed. It undermines town centres' distinctive appeal and character and gives the bystander the impression they could be anywhere. This disorientation is heightened by retailers' frequent re-invention of their corporate image and consequent introduction of new, integrated fascias, formats and product ranges. Rapidly evolving corporate strategies, frequent takeovers and mergers and ever-shorter product cycles are changing premises, shop names and facades at a rate which induces a sense of collective amnesia and lack of belonging (Worpole, 1992). These many subtle forms of sensory deprivation have appropriately been termed 'placelessness' (Relph, 1976). Commodification of the environment destroys the balance between continuity and change and promotes a narrow-minded consumerist mentality where customers choose where to shop solely on the basis of the range and price of goods and ease of purchase. If the social dimension to retailing continues to diminish in importance then town centres will suffer further damage as a result of competition from new retail locations and home shopping.

*Lack of public investment and comprehensive management*

Despite the many faults of the Victorian era, it did bequeath a legacy of grand gestures of civic spiritedness such as public squares and statues, town halls, museums, libraries, concert halls and parks. Many now provide a change of scene for shoppers and office workers and venues for evening entertainment. In contrast, few memorable public spaces or public buildings have been constructed in town centres over the last thirty years. Even in the interventionist 1960s and 1970s, the public realm lacked a custodian and champion. Landowners, developers, architects and engineers were primarily concerned with the design of buildings, structures and roads. Planners were responsible for disposition of land uses, reconciliation of the car and the pedestrian, individual planning applications and the preservation of historic buildings. Catering for rapid business expansion and rising car ownership was the priority and enhancement of civic spaces and buildings was of secondary importance. The overall design of the crucial spaces in-between buildings was neglected. Existing public open space was sacrificed to comprehensive redevelopment and road improvements. Squares such as Williamson Square, Liverpool, were split in two, turned into glorified traffic islands like Trafalgar Square, London, and in other instances obliterated altogether. Often civic quarters containing urban greenspace, libraries and museums became isolated from the remainder of the town centre by major roads. St John's Gardens in Liverpool was severed in this fashion from the remainder of the city centre.

During the 1980s, the situation deteriorated further. Cuts in government grants to local authorities and expenditure controls forced councils to cut maintenance budgets or sell-off public spaces. Worse still, many raided such budgets because local authorities are not statutorily obliged to maintain public open spaces nor do they receive grant support from central government. Private open space has also been lost because local authorities have not been sufficiently liquid to be able to compensate private owners for their inability to put the land to 'reasonable beneficial use'. Maintenance of pedestrianised areas and other public spaces has suffered from expenditure cuts. Only in prime retailing and office areas is there sufficient collective will amongst public and private sector interests to address such problems. While there have been occasional shining examples of local authorities investing in public facilities, these have usually been in relatively affluent areas (e.g. Centre Space, Hounslow; new museum, Croydon). Private philanthropy has failed to compensate for reductions in public expenditure.

Some responsibility for the decline in the public realm in town centres rests with the planning system. Since the influential Greater London Plan was produced by Abercrombie in 1943, it has become axiomatic to designate different land use zones, grouping them together in self-sufficient localities with transport corridors in between. Such compartmentalisation has reduced land use conflicts considerably, but has had two unfortunate consequences. First, zoning hastened the replacement of lower value industry, homes and cultural uses by high value office and retail uses in central areas.

Second, not enough thought was given to linkages between communities such as public open spaces and fringes of town centres. Consequently, much closer attention has been paid to traffic movement in the interstitial spaces than to enhancing the public realm. This has resulted in left-over public spaces which lack coherence or amenity value, especially in the disjointed transitional area between town centres and inner residential areas.

Public spaces demand strong, coherent management and policing as well as resources. They are prone to vandalism, graffiti and flyposting, litter and criminal acts against property. However, responsibility for the public realm is fragmented. Individual public or quasi-autonomous organisations act unilaterally and their actions often do not complement one another. Frequently streets are littered with a bewildering clutter of lamp posts, bollards, bins, traffic lights, street signs, telephone kiosks, control boxes. This leads to visual anarchy and loss of public amenity (Hillman, 1988).

*Opting out*

Parks departments are well aware of the way in which declining expenditure on care and supervision of public spaces triggers a downward spiral in their condition. Minimal maintenance of open space fails to check its mistreatment. The attendant vandalism, graffiti and litter deters older people, women and younger children. Increasing domination by young people further discourages others. Lack of money for imaginative refurbishment of such spaces offers little hope of reversing the downward slide. By contrast, out-of-centre retailing and leisure attractions such as multi-plex cinemas and bowling alleys and increasingly sophisticated forms of home entertainment offer perceivedly safer alternatives.

The general rise in criminal and anti-social activity in recent years has profoundly affected social attitudes and behaviour irrespective of the condition of the public realm. The British Crime Survey indicates that the total number of offences in England and Wales increased 36 per cent from about 11 to 15 million from 1981–91 whilst the population grew by only a negligible amount during the same period. Many people are increasingly reluctant to go out because of the combined fear of their homes being burgled, personal attack or robbery and damage to, or loss of, vehicles. It is also clear from crime surveys that a substantial proportion of the population feel so threatened by the prospect of personal attack or anti-social behaviour that they are reluctant to travel into town centres, especially at night.

However, town centres' shortcomings probably make such problems worse. Poorly designed and maintained public spaces increase fear of personal attack. Multi-storey car parks and underpasses soon become no-go areas. Poor lighting, the dominance of the pub culture and increased fear of attack on underused public transport services further discourage night-time visits to town centres.

Individual and corporate responses to the crime problem often make matters worse. The use of external roller shutters may protect individual properties effectively, but they may also deter self-policing, by discouraging window shopping after hours, and at the same time convey an impression that town centres are under siege. Close-circuit television cameras have proved successful in cutting shoplifting and petty theft but they may displace crime into unprotected areas. Private individuals' tendency to minimise risk of personal attack by using the car rather than taking the bus or walking, or alternatively staying at home, means that there are fewer people on the streets, which in turn encourages more criminal activity.

Fear of crime could contribute to a withdrawal into the home. The increasing cost of public transport and out-of-home entertainment relative to home entertainment may partially explain why poorer people spend an increasing amount of time at home (Bianchini, 1990). Similar shifts in the lifestyle of the affluent are more likely to be due to the rapid growth of home-based leisure pursuits such as gardening, computer games, home cinema, exercise machines. However, there may well be explanations common to all social groups such as the growth of satellite and cable TV. Home-based leisure pursuits have enabled people to escape from the public realm and retreat into their perceivedly safer, if sometimes artificial and predictable, private worlds. Town centres will have to be radically transformed to reverse such powerful social trends.

### *Signs of hope*

During the 1990s, however, there have been some encouraging developments. Growing professional awareness of the significance of the public realm has renewed interest in the cultural importance of town centres. Mono-functional areas and buildings have increasingly been rejected in favour of mixed use developments consisting of a livelier blend of residential, employment, leisure and cultural uses which can be utilised around the clock. The exodus of retail and office activity has forced once reluctant property interests to consider alternative uses, hence the success of the 'Living over the Shop' (LOTS) initiative and the appearance of other office-to-flat conversion schemes. Heightened competition from new retail locations has also prompted town centre interests to work more closely in partnership to improve standards of management and maintenance. Town centre managers have become a focus for public complaint and many have lobbied successfully for better cleansing regimes. In parallel, a talented set of urban designers have emerged who see themselves as guardians of the public realm rather than mere beautifiers of the urban landscape. These developments have generated a much greater awareness of the importance of designing public spaces so as to satisfy residents, shoppers and other users' emotional and practical needs. The main problem now is not the attitude of town centre interests and urban designers, but generating wider public usage and influencing large private corporations. The latter contribute little to the public realm because their own buildings are often predictable, uninspiring creations which have little relationship with individual localities.

## The future of the public realm in town centres

The future course of events will depend upon the attractiveness of town centres as retail locations, the degree to which ease of accessibility can be reconciled with environmental amenity and future patterns of social behaviour. The present situation is finely poised. Out-of-town retailing's market share is still increasing but the government has recently encouraged reinvestment in existing town centres. Traffic congestion worsens but car restraint is on everybody's agenda. Public spaces will probably continue to be grossly underfunded. Growing social polarisation, development of the Internet and increasing amounts of teleworking and tele-shopping all seem likely to diminish social contact. Escalation in street crime may result in the creation of physically distinct realms for elite core workers and for the more dispensible short-term contract workers and ghettoisation of the unemployed and poor. On the other hand, cities are back in fashion because they offer variety, excitement, cultural interest and vitality. Urban design is becoming more populist and town centre management, quality of life, liveability and sustainability will be urban policymakers' buzzwords for some time. Declining job mobility and growing constraints on personal mobility could heighten attachment to local centres. What are we to make of these seeming contradictions and what is the outcome likely to be?

Since town centres start from different points, they will follow different trajectories. Varying degrees of civic-mindedness and social responsibility, the level of appeal of cultural attractions and public and private patronage will make a critical difference. International comparisons confirm this. Although European and US town centres are similarly exposed to powerful global forces, their differing character emphasises the importance of civic culture and public policy. For example, the *Estate Romana* experiment in Rome in the late 1970s demonstrated that town centre regeneration involving a round-the-clock cultural entertainment, good lighting, and cheap public transport can be a powerful tool for revitalising the public realm (Bianchini, 1989).

All town centres will, none the less, have to cope with powerful economic and social forces. The most fundamental challenge will be how to cope with growing social polarisation, the fragmentation of value-systems and atomistic lifestyles created by heightened global economic competition and instant electronic communication. Social activity is growing more exclusivist, fragmented and segregated as a result of uneven economic development caused by unrestrained global business corporations, diminishing job opportunities and greater inequalities. Developments such as tele-cottages, bulletproof cars, and high security business parks with their own village greens suggest that wealthy elites are disengaging from the rest of society and escaping into private worlds. International elites are emerging which have more in common with their hypermobile foreign equivalents than their compatriots (Lasch, 1995).

While their appeal to students and the young will grow because they contain lively cultural activities and are centres of learning, there is little evidence that town centre interests will persuade a wider constituency to live, work and spend leisure time there rather than opt out of urban lifestyles. The main exceptions will be town centres with a rich architectural heritage of significant historic interest, or smaller town centres in commuter belts or semi-rural locations. Most local authorities will lack the resources or the powers to provide the support facilities to encourage families and the elderly to move back. There are few signs, for example, that cultural attractions of broad appeal are being developed within larger centres. Some 40 per cent of the population will be at or above retirement age by the year 2000 with different accommodation and healthcare needs; major opportunities are going to be missed if thought is not given to this situation now. Although urban regeneration is in vogue, a deeply-rooted anti-urban bias and a widely-held ideal of a home in the country will continue to influence residential preferences and how people spend their leisure time.

## Conclusion

Despite the advent of town centre management, shortages of rescoures will mean that the public realm in town centres will be vulnerable to conflicts between users, mistreatment by the public and appropriation by commercial interests. Strong public policies of protection and enhancement will be absolutely essential to the livelihood of the public realm. But given continuing decentralisation, social withdrawal and the lack of any territorial obligation of mobile international capita, more extreme measures will be necessary to reverse the decline. Something on the scale of the French 'Grands Projects' supported by a multiplicity of community-inspired projects might stimulate awareness of the advantages of urban lifestyles. Current political priorities and the narrow-mindedness of major business interests make this unlikely.

Under free market conditions, there is a constant danger that firms will appropriate and package the public realm to promote their products and boost profits, thereby destroying its intrinsic character and its potential to provide a platform for more spontaneous local cultural production and social activity. Equally, without substantial, well co-ordinated public investment and urban design by popular consent, the public realm is inevitably abused and its attractiveness undermined by anti-social activity. The long-term price of failing to care for the public realm is considerable for town centres. Finally, if public spaces which offer something for everyone are neglected and undervalued, what does that say about the future of our society? Two related marks of civilisation are the way a society treats its most vulnerable citizens and the degree to which all its citizens have equal access to its treasured institutions. In this respect the state of the public realm is crucial. But many people now doubt whether a public realm actually exists and would not automatically assume that town centres are a vital part of it. The lack of regard shown for public spaces and universal cultural facilities and meeting places is testimony to the decline in the nation's collective sense of social responsibility.

Despite this gloomy assessment, there is plenty of evidence from home and abroad that the public realm is not inevitably doomed to decline. Retailers' behaviour can make a difference. A leading New York bookshop encourages customers to browse for long periods by providing seating and remaining open until late in the evening. Networks of public spaces in Barcelona are well maintained and used at different times of the day by a wide cross-section of the community. Central Paris does not die in the evenings because a substantial number of well-off people live there and its variety of small, family-owned, shops partly reflects this. Achieving change is a question of political will, popular pressure and more enlightened social and business attitudes.

**References**

Abercrombie, P. and Forshaw, J.H, (1943) *County of London Plan*, London.

Beer A.R. (1991) 'Urban design: the growing influence of environmental psychology', *Journal of Environmental* Psychology, 11, pp. 359–71.

Bianchini, F. (1989) 'Cultural policy and urban social movements: the response of the 'New Left' in Rome (1976–85) and London (1981–86)', in Bramham P. *et al.* (eds) (1989).

Bianchini, F. (1990) 'The crisis of urban public social life in Britain: origins of the problem and possible responses', *Planning Policy and Research*, 5 (3) p. 4.

Biddulph, M. (1993) 'Design of the British city public realm: directing transition', Department of Civic Design, University of Liverpool.

Bramham, P. *et al.* (eds) (1989) *Leisure and Urban Processes: Critical Studies of Leisure Policy in West European Cities*, Routledge, London.

Civic Trust (1993) *Liveable Towns and Cities*, Report for Campaign for Liveable Places by European Institute for Urban Affairs, Liverpool John Moores University, Civic Trust, London.

Comedia (1991) *Out of Hours: a Study of Economic Social and Cultural Life in twelve town centres in the UK*, Comedia, London.

Department of Environment (1994) 'Vital and viable town centres: meeting the challenge', URBED *et al.*, HMSO, London.

Hayward, R. and McGlynn, S. (eds) (1993) *Making Better Places: Urban Design Now*, Butterworth-Heinemann, Oxford.

Herring Baker Harris and Intermarket Research (1995) 'The Cheshire retail study', Commission from Cheshire Local Planning Authorities, Herring Baker Harris.

Hillman, J. (1988) *A New Look for London*, report for Royal Fine Art Commission, HMSO, London.

Hubbard, P. (1993) 'The value of conservation. A critical review of behaviour research', *Town Planning Review*, 64 (4).

Lasch, C. (1995) *The Revolt of the Elites and the Betrayal of Democracy*, Norton Press, New York.

Lofland, L.H. (1989) 'The morality of urban public life: the emergence and continuation of a debate', *Places*, Fall.

Lynch, K. (1984) *Good City Form*, MIT Press, Cambridge, Massachussets.

Maslow, A.H. (1970) *Motivation and Personality*, Harper and Row, New York.

Montgomery, J. (1990) 'Cities and the art of public planning', *Planning Policy and Research*, 5 (3) p. 4.

Punter, J.V. (1990) 'The ten commandments of architecture and good design', *The Planner*, 5 (10), pp. 10–14.

Relph, R. (1976) *Place and Placelessness*, Pion, London.

Trench, S. *et al.* (1992) 'Safer cities for women: perceived risks and planning measures', *Town Planning Review*, 63 (3).

Worpole, K. (1992) *Towns for People*, Open University Press, Buckingham.

# Chapter 6
# Who shapes town centres?

## Introduction

Although the appearance and commercial livelihood of town centres is often debated, the agents and processes which shape the built environment are poorly understood. Most academic texts focus upon the quality of urban design or on particular specialist subjects such as transport, retailing or the development process. Yet the crucial question is who controls the town centres? The success of recent attempts to manage town centres will greatly depend upon properly understanding the levers of influence and the nature of the relationship between retailers, developers, local authorities, shoppers and other users. The subdued state of the property market presents an opportunity to reflect on which interests have most shaped town centres' evolution and whether recent changes have been in the wider public interest. A balance sheet of winners and losers will indicate where alternative policies are needed. The first section of the chapter profiles the key interests, explains why they are involved in town centres and their impact upon town centre environments. The next section explores the differing degrees of power and influence of particular interests and their varied methods of seeking control. Finally, the chapter ends by analysing the implications of the existing distribution of power.

## Who are the key interests?

Key interests may be divided into three main categories:

- *the producers* of town centre environments – such as property owners, developers, investors, retailers, construction and design professionals and informal producers such as buskers and pavement artists;

- *the users* – including occupants of buildings, and different users of town centres including employees, shoppers, residents, tourists and informal users;
- *the intermediaries* – including local and national government, estate agents, amenity organisations and pressure groups.

In practice, some organisations play a number of these roles. Nevertheless, the categorisation is useful in discriminating different motives for involvement in town centres.

One way of distinguishing producer interests is to visualise the different stages in the development process. All development requires initiators like landowners and developers, investors to provide capital and professional advisors to design, implement, let and manage schemes. Although this clarification minimises the significance of existing owners who have not been actively involved in the property market, it does focus upon the key agents of change – the primary theme of the chapter.

### *Land and property owners*

Patterns of land tenure in most town centres are extremely complex, reflecting the variety of constituent business activity and the differing property requirements and motives for ownership. Many businesses, especially the larger retailers and commercial organisations, purchase land or buildings and subsequently develop and occupy their own purpose-built premises. This gives them absolute control over their operating environment, security and independence. It is also a valuable source of collateral for bank loans and revenue. Alternatively, there are absentee landlords who sub-lease property to obtain a steady rental income. Since the First World War, the notion of retaining ownership of land and buildings for their current use value has been supplanted by the purchase of land as an investment to exploit its 'exchange value'. This may be achieved by refurbishment, change of use or redevelopment. Long-term commercial expansion of town centres, which gathered pace in the 1950s, has encouraged an increasing amount of speculative development, principally of offices and shops.

Prime property in major town centres has progressively fallen, for investment reasons, into the hands of pension funds, insurance companies and national and international banks. The scale of external ownership of town centre assets is not simply a reflection of an individual property's investment value but more fundamentally the dynamic nature and inherent unevenness of economic development and the increasing circulation of international capital constantly in search of the highest returns (Harvey, 1989). This is especially true of larger city centres.

Although external ownership of town centre property has grown, individual institutions seldom own more than a couple of properties in particular centres to spread their risks and maintain a balanced property portfolio (Whitehand, 1983). Together with the widespread practice of sub-leasing property for investment purposes, and fragmented local ownership, this has made concerted local action problematic. An extreme case was the failure to place a supplementary management charge upon owners and lessees of retail premises in Oxford Street, London, to fund improvements in environmental management because the chains of ownership were so extensive and complex that responsibilities could not be established (DoE, 1994). Increasing pressure upon local authority finance has also meant that local authorities can no longer use compulsory purchase powers to assemble land prior to redevelopment to the extent that they did in the 1960s.

The passive behaviour of many property owners has also proved problematic. Absentee landlords generally seek to maximise their income and minimise their legal obligations and calls upon their time. Larger investment organisations have devised an 'institutional lease' which places the majority of the maintenance and management responsibilities upon the tenant. Occupants are normally required to reassign the lease to another tenant if they vacate the accommodation. The lease also contains built-in rent review clauses which relate to the property's changing capital value rather than changes in the profitability of the business. Such terms effectively insulate land owners from short-term fluctuations in trading conditions and hence remove any incentive for them to be actively involved in schemes which promote town centres.

### *Developers*

Developers are an extremely heterogeneous group consisting of property companies, landowners, financial institutions, local authorities and public agencies, building contractors, construction companies and private occupiers, or combinations of them. While landowner and developer are one and the same in the case of new bespoke accommodation, property development companies perform a distinct role in the case of speculative development. Their wide range of tasks include assessment of market opportunities and potential clients' needs; site identification, inspection and assembly; arrangement of finance; commissioning architects and other designers; obtaining planning permission and management of professionals' contracts. Following completion of the development, they arrange for agents to let space to occupiers and manage the development and then either retain the property as collateral for other ventures, or sell it to another concern to obtain long-term finance.

Developers work closely with other property interests. Typically, property development companies have obtained finance either from a rolling programme of property development and sales or by entering into sale and leaseback deals with investment institutions or local authorities. The latter arrangement has proved particularly popular in town centres because of the scarcity and high cost of land. Such deals provide an immediate source of finance for the developer and in return a steady long-term income for investment institutions and local authorities. In the 1960s and 1970s, developers frequently entered into joint ventures with local authorities and pension funds on such a basis in order to undertake the comprehensive redevelopment of town centre retail and office areas. More recently, an increasing proportion of schemes have been supported by banks. However, the collapse of the property market in 1990, following a spectacular boom in largely bank-financed development, meant that property developers suffered from falling asset values, difficulties in letting and disposing of property and rising debt. This subsequently led to a wave of liquidations, and even major development companies such as Olympia and York, Mountleigh and Heron went bankrupt. Since that time developers have adopted a more cautious approach to property development and financing.

The behaviour and underlying motives of different developers vary considerably. Those constructing their own accommodation attach greater attention to special design requirements and fittings and to what extent the building will enhance company prestige and project its image. However, speculative development has become more important than the provision of bespoke accommodation. Speculative developers are principally concerned with the risk/reward balance and weigh excellence and sophistication of design against the outlay entailed. Although the building has to be functionally efficient and in the right location to make letting easy, the wish of developers to shorten construction time and secure early occupation of the building to minimise interest payments and maximise profits, militates against interesting and original design. Most developers will only pay for good design if it pays dividends in the short to medium term. Consequently, speculative development usually has less of a sense of individuality and character than bespoke accommodation. This kind of speculative activity usually damages the character of town centres because developers invariably seek to maximise rentable floor area, cut detail, and plagiarise and free-ride on other investments and designs. Unless public inducements and guarantees are available they will prefer prominent locations rather than difficult sites in less attractive fringe locations where there are added uncertainties. There are also public developers, such as local authorities, who are important providers of transport infrastructure such as car parks, as well as pedestrianised areas, seating areas, and public spaces which are crucial to town centres' attractiveness. Although they are able to use revenue from land and property sales for wider public purposes, their statutory obligation to maximise the value of property assets, coupled with limited resources and, often, a lack of flair, has resulted in poor design. In discussing developers and development it is easy to overlook internal changes to buildings which do not require planning permission. Retailers and other town centre businesses are important in this sense. The interiors of many town centre buildings have often been transformed to an even greater extent than their exteriors. The frequency of refits is increasing as businesses are taken over or change hands and firms repeatedly reinvent their corporate image in an attempt to appear more fashionable and innovative than their competitors.

*Property investors*

Investors are critical to the development process. They fall into two camps: those offering long-term finance and those providing short-term loans. Typically developers generate longer-term finance by selling completed developments to institutions or for owner occupation. Short-term finance is offered on a debt or an equity sharing basis. There are a multitude of methods of financing to suit the type of developer, the period over which finance is required and interest rate requirements. They originate mainly from three sources: bank loans, corporate finance and commercial mortgages.

Before the Second World War, most development was financed either by fixed rate mortgages or by the construction companies themselves. However, steady appreciation in capital values in desirable locations such as town centres prompted institutional involvement in property finance from the 1960s onwards. Insurance companies and pension funds became the most important sources of long-term finance in property but Property Unit Trusts and traditional institutions such as the Church Commissioners, universities and the Crown Estate also acquired significant assets. However, their appetite for such investment cooled in the 1980s because of low inflation, dramatic property slumps and higher returns from other forms of investment such as stocks and gilts and international property. By contrast, banks became increasingly important backers of property ventures in the latter part of the 1980s as the economy boomed as a consequence of deregulation, globalisation of capital markets and government fiscal policy. From 1985 to 1990, bank lending to property companies rose from £6.6 billion to £37.1 billion (Turok, 1992). Their emphasis upon supplying shorter-term, relatively expensive, loan finance to developers to cover land acquisition, design and construction costs, provided impressive immediate returns, but following the property collapse in 1990, many banks had to make heavy provision for bad debts. Since then they have been reluctant to invest in any but the safest schemes where income covers the interest on the loan.

Like developers, the institutions and banks are also concerned with the trade- off between the level of risk and the likely financial return. Pension funds are the most cautious and conservative in attitude, in view of their future obligations to pension holders. Consequently they target their investment upon relatively safe, state-of-the-art developments in prime, well-established town centre locations where there are good long-term prospects of occupancy by well-known and reliable tenants and minimal risk of the property being rendered obsolescent by technological innovations. The institutional lease has proved a further safeguard. Most institutional investment is channelled into prime areas of central London and major provincial cities with strong, diverse economies, freestanding market towns in growing regions, and other town centres with important assets such as historical buildings, tourist attractions and prestigious educational institutions. Large out-of-town shopping centres and business parks have also proved popular.

For a time in the late 1980s, banks showed a greater willingness to invest in more risky secondary as well as prime areas of town centres. However, recession and oversupply of floorspace meant that property companies suffered badly. Developers of non-prime town centre properties that have survived continue to face severe liquidity and long-term financial problems because, given sluggish market conditions, they are still struggling to lure owner occupiers. Generally, listed development companies are in a better position to be able to swap debt for equity finance and convert short-term loans into long-term securities. The ability of institutions and equity investors to pick and choose between a large number of properties has reinforced the gap in popularity between prime and secondary areas of town centres in investment terms. Hence the best town property has been creamed off by externally based institutions and secondary property is increasingly avoided. Domestic property development is now just one element in a balanced international portfolio of investments, each with different risk/reward profiles so as to maximise security of return in the long term (Berry *et al.*, 1993).

*Construction and design professionals*

While some interests are commissioned to deal with specific aspects of the production process, the visual impact of their contribution can be considerable and lasting. Architects, construction companies, shopfitters, consulting engineers and interior designers all fall into this category. The level and sophistication of design input depends upon the client, the location of the building and the attitude of the design professional. Purpose-built accommodation in prime areas of town centres is generally constructed by large professional firms operating on a national scale. Conversely, the design element is likely to be less marked in the case of speculative schemes. Developers involved in projects in secondary areas may be tempted to cut costs because of tighter margins by employing contractors on a design-and-build basis where the design input is negligible. In all of these instances, respect for context, local detailing and attention to users' needs or aspirations are often overlooked.

Professional attitudes sometimes explain why some town centre schemes relate to and enhance their surroundings less than others. Frequently, more attention is given to meeting the technical requirements of the brief and the making or preservation of reputations than to wider issues of urban design and the necessity to involve all partners, including amenity groups, in the process. Often the design of individual buildings and the spaces between are completely divorced from one another. Consequently urban designers have great difficulty tidying up the visual mess.

*Informal producers*
There are other often unrecognised 'producers' of 'soft' town centre environments who play a crucial role in creating a sense of place. These include buskers, pavement artists, street market sellers and participants in street events and festivals. Such groups and individuals are becoming more important in maintaining and enhancing the distinctiveness of particular towns as the production of the built environment is increasingly concentrated in fewer hands and standardised design solutions become the rule and the number of locally owned businesses dwindles. However, some of these producers are itinerant and have only a transitory impact. And while some people regard them as entertainers, others see them as a nuisance.

*Users*
Users include the most wide ranging set of individuals and interests. The word 'user' is preferred to 'consumer' which implies organisations or individuals purchasing goods and services such as property, retail goods and professional advice. This excludes non-monetary transactions like experiencing the general ambience of a town centre, window-shopping and meeting friends which are also important. Employees' quality of life is a mixture of both of these aspects of consumption. Users in the wider sense include occupants of buildings, employees, shoppers, residents, visitors and informal users.

The nature of consumption and the needs, attitudes and aspirations of the user are a reflection of differing cultural values, preferences, and individuals' age, social class and ethnic background. Depending upon the time, place and type of consumption, individual preferences can shift. Shoppers may opt for the supermarket which is guaranteed to offer value for money, convenience, reliability and accessibility if they are in a rush, whereas if they have more time on their hands they may comparison shop. Many subtle tradeoffs exist between price of goods and the quality and location of retail environments. Increasingly, there is an inverse relationship between the amount of disposable income and the time available to spend it. The poor tend to be 'time-rich' and the rich 'time-poor'.

This diversity generates representational and ownership problems. Defining users' interests is far from straightforward. If there is a conflict of interest, should permanent residents' or constituent businesses' interests be regarded as more important than visitors' and shoppers'? Should preferential treatment be given to car-borne shoppers in view of their economic importance or should precedence be given to 'green modes' such as walking, cycling and public transport? In the face of such difficulties, the main agents of change are sometimes tempted to act unilaterally using gut instinct or conviction rather than following exhaustive consultation. However, such actions carry the risk that users' shared motivations and requirements are overlooked. The relationship of proposed development to existing buildings and the neighbouring environment is, for example, of much wider concern (Groat, 1986). More generally, common denominators do exist. Personal safety, association, identification and sense of belonging, accessibility, distinctive place identity, personal service, variety of street scene, range not only of shops but variety of cultural attractions and places to meet matter a great deal to the majority of users. Many tourist and arts attractions, for instance, are a shared asset between residents, shoppers, visitors and town centre workers.

*Intermediary organisations*

An important set of intermediary interests occupies the middle ground between producers and users. These include local and national government, estate agents, lobby and amenity groups. Their precise roles differ and can include guardianship, consultation, coordination, advocacy, bargaining and reconciliation. Local authorities largely adopt a custodial role. They identify and fill gaps in infrastructure such as providing additional car parking and tourist facilities, often acting in an enabling rather than direct capacity. They counteract market failure by using pump-priming mechanisms such as fiscal incentives, guarantees and infrastructural provision. They use land use and design controls to provide greater certainty or scarcity value for developers and investors. Generally they promote the centre's attractiveness by enhancing maintenance regimes, supporting campaigns, street-events and festivals.

The degree of local authority commitment to town centres can vary considerably. Manifestly, some have a vested interest in pursuing regeneration measures since they are often substantial town centre landowners themselves. But town centres often lack political significance. They contain few residents and expenditure in them lacks the immediacy of impact in electoral terms compared with financial support for services which affect residential areas directly. Also the introduction of the unified business rate has lessened accountability to town centre businesses. Overall, expenditure constraints limit what can be done and make local authorities reluctant to direct expenditure away from local services. In this situation the degree of long-term vision and the leadership and tenacity of prominent elected members and officers often determines whether town centre projects are actively supported. Similarly, local authorities' ability to compete for increasingly discretionary supplementary funding sources, such as City Challenge, can be critical in deciding whether they can realise such ambitions.

In the past, local authorities have been criticised by town centre businesses on the grounds of departmentalism, low standards of service, especially given high rates charges and failure to address infrastructural weaknesses and users' needs. Given this lack of legitimacy and the need to respond to the threat of greater competition from out-of-town locations and other centres, an increasing number of local authorities, town centre businesses and other interests have unilaterally or in partnership, appointed town centre managers. Their principal virtue is their impartiality, a clear territorial responsibility, continuous availability and ability to act as a sounding-board for all parties. Their duties usually include co-ordination of efforts to promote the centre, mediation between producer and user interests, lobbying for additional expenditure and ensuring that the town centre is efficiently managed. They are enablers rather than doers since they rarely exercise direct control over a substantial capital budget.

Two other intermediary organisations merit special mention. First, there are the larger estate agents who now perform a much broader role than simply letting space. They are involved with most aspects of the property market such as buying and selling, market research, advice on investment opportunities and estate management. Like local authorities, they have a vested interest in buoying up town centre property markets and are therefore heavily involved in town centre management initiatives and attempts to raise publicity about the plight of town centres. In practice, however, they hedge their bets like many retailers and are frequently involved in promoting out-of-town business locations which potentially undermine town centres. Second, particular interests have established lobby groups in some town centres to advance their cause. Prime examples include umbrella groups representing business or conservation and various amenity groups fighting major redevelopment schemes, pedestrianisation proposals and revised access arrangements.

*Relationships between key interests*

Before attempting to establish which organisations have the most powerful influence upon shaping town centre environments, it is useful to picture the network of relationships between the different individuals and organisations involved. Both the frequency of contact and the strength of bond can vary significantly. Links between producers are strong and intense and mainly centre upon the developer. They are however episodic in nature because they focus on particular construction projects. Landowners tend to have little contact with other town centre organisations, their disinterest stemming from security of income, given institutional leases, and because an increasing proportion are absentee landlords. Most producers have considerable dealings with intermediaries such as local authority planning and highway departments, property agents and town centre managers. Typically, these concern approval of planning applications, letting and management of property and general promotion of the town centre. Significantly, links with different users are not strong. The main exception is the indirect link between property owners and their occupants, via property agents.

Users are a distinctive category in that they have virtually no direct dealings with each other except contact between businesses and their employees on such matters as transport and access arrangements. Most consumers relate to each other only indirectly through participation in lobby groups or approaches to town centre managers over particular issues. Unilateral links to intermediary organisations are dense, if episodic. They relate to particular concerns such as responding to planning applications or common problems such as lack of amenities, litter and graffiti. Relationships with producers are not well developed and mostly centre upon either lobbying the local authority to carry out infrastructural improvements, response to consultation on planning applications or real estate matters such as rental terms and lease agreements. Shoppers do relate to retailers but mainly over particular products rather than on the more general issue of the retail environment. Interestingly, users have a narrow role, despite their pivotal significance.

Intermediary organisations lie at the heart of most networks. Local authorities are closely involved with both producers and consumers in deciding on the appropriate use of land and buildings, highway arrangements and maintenance regimes. Increasingly though, town centre managers have become the point of contact on daily issues of concern to users. They also work closely with other intermediaries such as local authorities, property agents and lobby groups in resolving infrastructural difficulties, co-ordinating promotional campaigns and building consensus and commitment. Property agents play an increasingly important role in liaising between landowners, developers and tenants and more generally representing property interests.

This analysis suggests that most relationships revolve around individual property matters or particular issues rather than around general issues of common concern. Yet in both cases, the relationships are episodic. The analysis also shows that many organisations one would expect to wield influence, like landowners, investors and resident businesses (except retailers), are relatively disengaged. They have few linkages with other town centre interests. Only now that widespread concern about town centres' commercial prospects is being expressed is there emerging evidence that users' concerns are being taken more seriously and that dialogue between different interests is becoming more structured and sustained.

The limited nature of the dialogue also implies that the capacity of different interests to initiate and control the terms of debate varies. Producers such as landowners, public and private developers and investors largely set the agenda by developing schemes to which other interests then respond. Generally, specialised professional groupings which have developed their legitimacy by obtaining statutory powers, such as highway engineers and planners, have a much greater ability to intervene than other professionals with only informal influence, such as urban designers and the general public (McGlynn, 1993).

### *The distribution of power*

Town centres are perpetually in a state of flux as a result of constantly shifting liaisons and confrontations between sets of interests with fundamentally different motives. They can be places of competition or collaboration, conflict or compromise, contradiction or common celebration. Some interests repeatedly dominate others however and profoundly alter the nature of town centre environments.

Generally, producers, like landowners and investors, have dominated user interests because they control the key assets and initiate physical change. This applies particularly in the prime areas of town centres where externally-based institutional landlords have creamed off the very best real estate in return for supplying developers with long-term finance. Such external interests have subsequently placed exacting demands upon tenants in the knowledge that, in the event of their defaulting, they will have to reassign the tenancy under the terms of the lease. In the event of bankruptcy, given the pivotal position of such sites, the institutions know there are likely to be other takers. A combination of factors including land-use zoning and controls upon building heights has sustained the scarcity value of such real estate, which, coupled with high construction and refurbishment costs, have driven up values and business overheads in the remainder of the town centre. In addition, the replacement of the local rates system with a uniform national business rate has meant that local charges cannot reflect variation in local circumstances or business turnover and confidence. All these factors have placed a heavy burden upon business occupants and weakened their ability to survive. Bluntly, property has been overvalued and overrated while wealth production has been unduly penalised. Worse still, an undue proportion of the wealth of the most successful local companies has been siphoned off by external interests, rather than ploughed back into town centre economies. In environmental terms, such external control of production has resulted in buildings which are solidly built but lack flair and individuality and local detail or interest.

Investors also exercise control over other producers. Developers are vulnerable to investors suddenly moving out of property if its projected rate of return falls relative to other forms of investment. After the property collapse in 1990, many developers were placed in great difficulty because institutions pressed for discounts in property values and were increasingly reluctant to purchase any but the best properties. Major British and overseas banks also possess considerable clout and power. The majority have survived the latest property slump, even though many have had to absorb the costs of a large number of imprudent loans to development companies which went bankrupt. The banks have effectively compensated for bad property debts by increasing their charges dramatically and pulling out of all but the safest forms of property lending.

Design professionals are in a subservient position because they are answerable to their contractual masters. A series of factors have progressively weakened the position of professionals like architects, apart from a minority who have cult status. First, mounting criticism of modern architecture, coupled with the architectural and planning disasters of the 1960s, damaged their reputation and credibility. Second, design professionals have been vulnerable to the extreme upswings and downswings of the construction cycle. High levels of unemployment have affected their status. Third, designs have generally become more routine because of the growth of speculative rather than bespoke construction, the growing dominance of large clients wishing to project a consistent corporate image and the introduction of cost-cutting methods in the face of the prolonged recession and limits upon public expenditure. Efficiency savings have been achieved principally by the use of off-the-shelf designs, cheaper materials and the employment of contractors on design-and-build contracts.

Not all initiators of development are in a strong bargaining position. Landlords and developers with property holdings in secondary areas have either had to sit tight and hope that prospective tenants will eventually materialise or discount heavily if short-term capital is needed. Similarly, many developers have been exposed to downturns in the property market because they undertook property transactions and completed new development when the market had passed its peak. User interests have again found themselves on the receiving end of their actions. On some occasions speculative developers have constructed overspecified properties whose fixtures have subsequently been ripped out because they did not suit user requirements. Violent swings in the property market have promoted a herd-like instinct amongst developers which is no substitute for proper market research. Too often the end result has been waste.

Users' status is partly dependent upon spending power. Those users with the financial means have carried greater influence than informal users of town centres, partly because retailers are such a powerful lobby and partly because the importance of public institutions responsible for the social fabric of town centres has diminished. The size of user organisation also makes a critical difference. Large retailers and other service sector companies have a number of inherent advantages over smaller organisations. They are more able to purchase and construct buildings for owner occupation which can be dovetailed to their operational requirements. Major retailers can also adopt a strong bargaining stance when developers are initially seeking to attract 'anchor' stores into new shopping precincts to ensure the viability of the remaining, smaller, retail units. Consequently, they can insist on the best trading position and negotiate favourable occupancy terms. This also applies when developers of large speculative office schemes attempt to woo major commercial organisations in order to underpin the venture. The rating system also favours larger concerns. Major retailers enjoy relatively low overheads because the unit cost per square foot of rateable floorspace falls when a greater amount of floorspace is owned or leased. Favourable overheads and economies of scale enable large retailers to provide a wide range of retail goods cheaply. Increasing sales volumes have enabled retail chains to extend their dominance further by making bulk purchases, thus dictating product requirements to manufacturers and dispensing with wholesalers. Many small retailers cannot compete on these terms and inevitably go to the wall.

Although the customer is regarded as king in a retailing sense, the scale and ubiquity of advertising and marketing implies that user behaviour can be steadily manipulated to retailers' ends. The commercialisation of heritage, the successful infiltration of the tourism industry by 'leisure retailing' and the commodification of lifestyles, for example using designer labels, so that young people increasingly categorise each other according to what they possess, suggests that producers dominate users, provided they offer reasonable service and value for money. However, there is growing evidence that large retailers will need to be careful. User opinion about environmental issues such as car dependency, unethical practices, standardisation of product labels and also displacement of small community-based businesses by national retail chains is already provoking a backlash. Boycotting of particular stores and goods as a form of protest has become more common recently.

Most categories of town centre users are in a weak bargaining position because they are a fragmented constituency with diverse views, whose opinions are only formally sought in relation to particular building proposals. Until the advent of town centre management very recently, mechanisms for promoting popular debate about town centre environments have been lacking. Although local authorities have long exercised a guardianship role, excessive departmentalism, expenditure cuts, and, with a few exceptions, a half-hearted commitment to town centres have militated against coherent local debate and the proper engagement of a variety of user interests.

Over the last decade the position of intermediaries has strengthened as concern has grown about the quality of town centre environments and their future. Many local authorities have increasingly realised, if belatedly, that town centres are a major economic, social and cultural asset. This pro-growth attitude has provided a popular rallying point for most interests and given intermediaries added legitimacy. There is however a risk that intermediaries like local authorities and estate agents, will align themselves with producer rather than user interests since the former are more influential and more directly affect the quality of the physical environment.

*The importance of context and economic circumstances*

General economic conditions and swings in the property cycle can either heighten conflict or improve relations between interests by placing some in a stronger position than others. Recessionary conditions appear to induce greater conflict. Overheads and external costs do not adjust sufficiently rapidly to reflect the downturn in business turnover and, as a result, town centre businesses can suddenly face crippling burdens. The institutional lease, the uniform business rate and also indirect costs such as higher public transport fares and increased car parking charges are the principal culprits.

Intermediaries, such as local authorities, face many additional pressures to comply with producer interests in depressed economic circumstances. Developers operating on tight margins often submit plans on a take-it-or-leave-it basis knowing that the local authority will be loath to turn away any development which promises jobs and gives it kudos. There is the danger of any development being viewed as good development. In such circumstances urban design issues can easily become a dispensable luxury and the harmful effects of new development upon neighbouring businesses or other retail centres overlooked.

Rifts also open up between producer interests in recessionary conditions. Banks on the one hand have a vested interest in propping up property values since they often accept property as collateral on their loans to developers. Indeed banks often accept bricks and mortar as security for non-property loans, too. To avoid a crash in values they tend to exercise patience with borrowers experiencing cashflow difficulties by rescheduling repayments. On the other hand, institutions contemplating property investment and desiring longer-term appreciation in value will press for heavy discounts in property values if they think that current book values are excessively high. Developers face a difficult dilemma trying to satisfy both camps. Frequently, they offer concessions to tenants by easing rent charges, and relaxing rent reviews and lease clauses in order to boost lettings income and ease bank repayments. Such moves tend, however, to alienate investors and reduce investment values and the prospects of making a decent return on disposal. Substantial discounts in rentals and freeholds have offered some compensation for businesses struggling with lack of demand in recessionary conditions. This is especially true of towns where there is an acute oversupply of accommodation and also in hard-to-let fringe areas of town centres. This advantage applies more to businesses which are able to move than to sitting tenants.

Many of the tensions can only be resolved if interests exercise a collective determination to reverse commercial decline and social disintegration. Secular decline produces disintegration but the prospect of revival and renewed prosperity encourages integration. This probably explains why there has been such broad-based support for the concept of town centre management (TCM). External threats in the form of out-of-town shopping and decentralisation of commercial activity have tended to bring together often conflicting interests to promote town centres. In contrast with the fragmentation previously described, TCM has resulted in the pooling of increasingly scarce resources, a broader exchange of ideas for enhancing a centre's attractiveness by blending commercial expertise with local authority perspectives and powers and offering a means for users to express their opinions.

The experiences in the late 1980s show that an overheated economy and a booming property market can cause great problems, too. Property owners charge vastly inflated rentals, and if redevelopment is pending, landowners hold out for higher prices which reduces the rate for the developer. Space users end up paying inflated rents as the developer passes on some of the increased development costs. Given the problems and tensions associated with pronounced upswings and downswings in economic circumstances and the property market, the achievement of steady economic growth is a necessity for the regeneration of town centres.

## Conclusion

The attractiveness of town and city centres depends critically upon the extent to which producers of the built environment make buildings and spaces which reflect the range of tastes and aspirations as well as the practical requirements and needs of their users. Although this is as much a question of aesthetics as of producing efficient and functional buildings, most British town centres have been filled with buildings short on visual appeal and cultural value. This is largely a reflection of the undue dominance of producer interests over user interests. The activities of largely externally-based property interests has proved disastrous for town centre environments. Such interests see property as an investment and, lacking any sense of territorial affinity, remain blissfully unaware of local culture or what matters to town centre users in the broader sense. Much town centre development has tended to be out of keeping with the existing fabric and lacking in local detail. National retail chains, for example, show little regard for the way in which their superstores destroy the character of smaller town centres whose High Streets consisted of mainly small retailers. Long-term social assets have been placed too much in the hands of powerful producer interests whose awareness of local cultural values and respect for history is minimal (Whitehand, 1983).

The growing disillusionment with the state of town centres is the ultimate verdict upon the way producer interests have exploited such areas for their own ends and opened up equally banal but more convenient developments in out-of-town locations. Ironically, user opinion is the most powerful long-term influence of all because it can lead to the virtual abandonment of the High Street. Despite the fragmented nature and limited influence of user interests, the growth of ethical shopping and the boycott of supermarkets on environmental grounds does suggest that orchestrated and well informed user action could hold producers more immediately to account in future. TCM may bring together producer and user concerns in new ways and engender broader debates about town centres' future. Whether this, on its own, will result in the necessary shifts in the balance of power is doubtful. For that to happen much more radical policies will be needed. The final chapter suggests a way forward.

## References

Berry, J. *et al.* (eds) (1993) *Urban Regeneration, Property Investment and Development*, E. & F.N. Spon, London.

Davies, R.L. and Champion, A.G. (eds) (1983) *The Future for the City Centre*, Institute of British Geographers Special Publication 14, Academic Press, London, pp. 41–59.

Department of Environment (1994) 'Vital and viable town centres: meeting the challenge', URBED *et al.*, HMSO, London.

Groat, L.N. (1986) 'Contextual compatibility: a study of meaning in the urban environment', unpublished paper presented to the Annual Meeting of the Association of American Geographers, Minneapolis.

Harvey, D. (1989) *The Urban Experience*, Basil Blackwell, Oxford.

Hayward, R. and McGlynn, S. (eds) (1993) *Making Better Places: Urban Design Now*, Butterworth-Heinemann, Oxford.

McGlynn, S. (1993) 'Reviewing the rhetoric', in Hayward, R. and McGlynn, S. (eds) (1993).

Turok, I. (1992) 'Property led urban regeneration: panacea or placebo', *Environment and Planning – A*, 24 (3), pp. 361–79.

Whitehand, J.W.R. (1983) 'Land-use structure, built-form and agents of change', in Davies, R.L. and Champion, A.G. (1983).

# Chapter 7
# Public policy – for better, for worse?

## Introduction

In the post-war period there have been pronounced shifts in the way town centres have been administered locally. Changes in public policy at a national level have also been important. Following heavy public criticism, the comprehensive physical restructuring of the 1960s gave way to more passive, protectionist policies in the 1970s. Increasingly *laissez-faire* policies in the 1980s led to concerns about competition from new outlying centres of business activity and this provoked another change of tack. Current policies advocate concentration of development within town centres and their active promotion and management. This chapter charts these changes in direction and seeks to explain the many volte-faces, inconsistencies and contradictions in policy-making. It also assesses the relative impact of different policy phases upon town centres' economy, accessibility, appearance and social character.

The chapter begins by recalling the main features of earlier phases of policy-making, assesses their legacies and highlights the reasons for successive changes. Later sections assess the new orthodoxies of active management and enhancement of town centres' commercial role. The chapter concludes by questioning whether public policy has reflected and accommodated economic and social changes or accentuated or modified events. The emphasis is on philosophies and broader strategies as policy specifics have been dealt with in the thematic chapters.

## Brave new world (1960s)

Before the late 1950s, most British town centres had evolved slowly with the exception of those strategically important towns and cities requiring extensive reconstruction as a result of Second World War bombing. Dramatic changes were in the offing, however. Growing prosperity, demands for modern office space, the increasing number and size of retailers and growth in car ownership was rapidly rendering the existing fabric obsolete. Congestion was mounting and the conflict between pedestrians and vehicles was becoming increasingly serious. The seminal Buchanan Report 'Traffic in Towns' in 1963 warned that, failing intervention, town centres would soon be unable to cope with access demands given the projected escalation in car ownership (HMSO, 1963). The policy solution devised by architects and planners – comprehensive redevelopment – was a logical one. The strategy was to extend retail and office areas, segregate pedestrians and vehicles by constructing subways and high level walkways and improve accessibility through road construction and the encouragement of public transport. Armed with compulsory purchase powers granted in the 1947 Town and Country Planning Act, local authorities acquired considerable amounts of property and, in partnership with a growing army of property developers, eagerly refashioned town centre environments. Extensive demolition of inner area slums offered planners, engineers and architects the opportunity to implement modernist thinking on a grand scale. Town centre ring roads and spurs were developed to remove through-traffic and to direct motorists to multi-storey car parks in distinctive office and retail zones to minimise land use conflicts. In neighbouring inner areas, high-rise flats were erected and surrounded by open space through which public super-highways were routed. A number of towns and cities introduced innovative solutions for public transport such as private–public transport interchanges. Redevelopment soon became a symbol of civic pride as towns vied with each other to be the first to open new purpose-built shopping precincts and labyrinthine walkways. In some cases, developers discussed schemes directly with politicians and bypassed the planners altogether.

The initial bout of hope and enthusiasm for the advent of a brave new world soon gave way to public dismay. Comprehensive redevelopment policies proved increasingly unpopular because they destroyed cherished town centre buildings and landmarks and closed long-established businesses. The undistinguished character of new buildings with their cold, brutalist facades of concrete and glass poured salt on the wounds. Many local authorities lost public confidence because they seemed to be in league with rapacious property developers who overdeveloped central sites by exploiting loopholes in planning legislation. Local authorities' planning solutions turned out to be flawed, conceptually and practically. The segregation of cars and people proved expensive and unpopular. Pedestrians were reluctant to use subways and walkways because of the fear of being mugged. They found switching level inconvenient, disorientating and unappealing. Essentially, pedestrians were having to make way for motorists. Replacement of areas of mixed use with mono-functional land use zones produced dead environments outside opening hours. These have proved socially undesirable and inefficient in terms of energy consumption. Overzealous clearance and replacement of traditional terraced housing with council flats and maisonettes re-emphasised the depopulation of inner areas. More static fringe areas were largely untouched, incongruously sandwiched between the extensively redeveloped central and inner urban areas.

The rapid transformation of town centres in the 1960s was the result of economic growth in a heady atmosphere of consumerism and policy makers' regrettable idealism and collective confidence in their ability to forge a modern environment. But the dreams turned sour and few have mourned the passing of wholesale redevelopment and the demise of autocratic 'evangelistic bureaucrats'. Technocratic solutions to the challenges of slum conditions and urban congestion proved widely unpopular. Policies largely consisted of the physical accommodation of economic realities at the expense of enhancing town centres' social value (Holliday, 1983). Design solutions were often wrongly conceived, hurried, and often used unproven and subsequently unpopular materials. Many town centres have since been saddled with the social and financial consequences of remedying decisions made in the 1960s.

## The switch to conservation (1970s)

In the 1970s the mood changed sharply. The oil crisis halted economic growth, the property market collapsed, 'stagflation' confounded the economists and public finances progressively deteriorated. The emphasis upon comprehensive redevelopment gave way to a quieter period of management and refurbishment. In the office sector, for example, growth in floorspace continued but the pace of development was slacker than in the previous decade due to oversupply, slower overall growth, decline in public employment and opposition to large schemes in residential areas. The same economic conditions affected retailing although large-scale shopping centres were built in some major city centres, such as the Victoria Centre, Nottingham, and Eldon Square, Newcastle. Towards the end of the decade, however, the economy began to improve and growing consumer spending led to additional retail development, especially new superstores, either on amalgamated central sites or in edge-of-town locations.

Slower economic growth and more incremental policies went hand in hand. Limited provision was made for further expansion of offices. Retail policies sought to protect the existing hierarchy and town centres' role for higher order retailing. But since the need for new retail space was linked to demographic and employment trends, the amount of new development was modest by previous standards. Developments in transport were also comparatively unspectacular and included a limited amount of pedestrianisation and provision of bus priority lanes rather than extensive new infrastructure. Although local authorities continued to subsidise public transport heavily, most were reluctant to implement stringent controls upon car parking and undertake extensive pedestrianisation, worried they might upset commercial interests, deter new investment or reduce existing custom.

In retrospect, the 1970s was a strangely dormant phase in public policy-making, best summed up as a cautious muddling through. The consequences of growing car ownership were largely overlooked or underestimated. Little progress was made in restricting car usage and developing alternative modes. Similarly, local authorities gave scant attention to whether existing retail space was becoming outmoded, despite the emergence of new forms of retailing such as superstores and retail warehouses. In the wider context, no attempt was made to link the economic potential of town centres as locations for expanding business services firms with the increasing needs of surrounding inner areas, even though awareness of inner city problems was growing.

Explanations for this passivity are difficult to disentangle. Slower growth, the reaction against the excesses of the 1960s, the growing influence of the conservation lobby and restrictions in local authority expenditure and hence use of compulsory purchase powers all contributed. Political developments also played a part: local government reorganisation in 1974 led to tensions between the new upper and lower tiers, especially in metropolitan areas, and to delays and uncertainties since both had responsibilities in town centres. In most localities, however, production of town centre plans was delayed pending approval of County Structure Plans.

The lack of connection between town centre planning and inner city policies stemmed from the concentration of grant assistance and environmental improvements in discrete areas, the embryonic state of economic development mechanisms, like training and marketing, and the physical orientation of the planning system with its inability to influence land usage positively. Moreover, local authorities increasingly believed that town centres were capable of looking after themselves and that they should focus upon more pressing problems elsewhere. However, this reordering of priorities does not explain why fringe areas of town centres – typically occupied by marginal or declining economic activities and often blighted by sporadic redevelopment, road proposals and slum clearance – continued to be neglected despite becoming increasingly incoherent and run down. This further emphasised the dislocation in spatial policies.

However, the 1970s did witness some positive developments. Given the urgent need to generate more jobs, town centre plans made greater provision for maintaining a mix of employment functions by designating zones for more traditional industries. More generally, the growth of the conservation movement led to a raft of legislation in the late 1960s and early 1970s empowering local authorities to claim government grant aid to refurbish housing in General Improvement Areas and Housing Action Areas. Authorities could also designate areas of architectural or historic interest as conservation areas and control demolition and alterations in such localities. As a result, considerable sums of money were spent on refurbishing those town centres which had a fine heritage of buildings. Increasing concern and interest in environmental issues meant that the preservation of heritage features within town centres was complemented by additional tree planting and the protection and enhancement of important civic spaces and buildings.

Overall, policy-making in the 1970s lacked a grasp of emerging economic dynamics and the positive means to fashion commercial revival in town centres. Zoning and physical refurbishment provided a framework, even an attractive context. However, local planners' and politicians' aspirations for employment generation lacked substance because the necessary public sector lead was not forthcoming. Slower economic growth and a concern not to cause further public outcry became an excuse for passive policy-making, bordering on complacency.

### Progressive deregulation and promotion of economic development (1980s)

The change of government in 1979 heralded a more *laissez-faire* style of governance which had profound implications for town centres. The Thatcher government maintained that deregulation of public sector controls was necessary because they held back private sector investment. It insisted that the private sector could best decide about the nature and location of development. Consumers would also benefit from more open and intensive competition. Public expenditure was deemed too high and to be crowding out private sector investment and was consequently cut sharply. The White Paper 'Lifting the Burden' typified the new philosophy by exhorting public servants, including planning professionals, to be more favourably inclined to development (DoE, 1985). In the same vein, Circular 22/80 advised local planning authorities that there should normally be a presumption in favour of development, unless clear reasons for refusal could be given (DoE, 1980).

This change of philosophy placed many local authorities in an ambiguous position. On the one hand, their previous style of governance was now criticised for being prescriptive, heavy handed and interventionist. But on the other, they were exhorted to adopt an enabling role to deal with market failure. Many became frustrated that their diminished status and powers made them unable to respond properly to growing local pressure to promote economic development, particularly where new private sector investment was manifestly failing to compensate for heavy job losses in traditional industries. Not surprisingly, differences of approach to economic development soon emerged which were to affect town centres.

National policies were oriented towards the removal of physical and institutional constraints facing the private sector. Government believed that overly burdensome planning controls, local government bureaucracy and political interference, excessive land reclamation or building refurbishment costs, environmental degradation and inadequacies in public infrastructure all contributed to the lack of private sector confidence. Enterprise Zones, Urban Development Corporations, and fiscal mechanisms such as the Urban Development Grant were all born of that logic. To the extent that government policy had a territorial focus, most of their spatially targeted initiatives lay outside town centres. Only occasionally, and indirectly, did government initiatives benefit town centres because of their physical proximity.

Local authority economic development policies by contrast were more wide-ranging and interventionist. They included traditional measures such as grant support for firms in priority areas and servicing of land and buildings. These were later supplemented by a wide range of business support services, training initiatives, technology transfer schemes and the promotion of inward investment. While the majority of these measures were widely applied, town centres' growing importance as tourism and arts venues made them the focus of sectoral policies. Local policymakers realised that urban tourism, embracing arts festivals, business conferences, exhibitions and mini-hotel breaks, was becoming an important economic activity. Theatre, music, painting and sculpture, and contemporary cultural industries such as film, video, broadcasting, electronic music, publishing, design and fashion were also concentrated in central locations. Local authorities were also increasingly aware that these attractions could prove decisive in attracting footloose inward investment. Some authorities sought to channel such activity into refurbished historic quarters because of the growing appreciation of urban heritage and its tourist appeal.

Tourist activity in town centres was promoted by offering financial support for the development of new attractions, improvements in visitor facilities and provision of support services like marketing and training. Authorities sought to capitalise upon the economic importance of the arts by supporting local arts festivals to promote local talent, strengthen civic identity and pride and enliven social life in the town centre. They used sculpture and good design as a means of beautification and image building and channelled public moneys into distinct cultural quarters to concentrate and combine cultural production and consumption activities. Often the local authority provided marketing, management advice and training infrastructure in addition to suitably designed buildings. Prime examples of this were the Cultural Quarter, Sheffield, the Media Quarter,

Digbeth (Birmingham), Nottingham Lace Quarter and Little Germany in Bradford. Birmingham City Council was particularly effective in orchestrating a number of different sources of grant assistance including Urban Programme moneys, Urban Development Grant and Derelict Land Grant, and European grants in order to renovate the historic Jewellery Quarter of its city centre. Some authorities responsible for administering historic town centres set up Town Schemes which enabled them to use English Heritage funds to refurbish shopfronts, facades and streetscapes. Far-sighted authorities revised their town centre strategies and plans to weld the promotion of economic sectors and distinctive quarters with the development of the remainder of the core area in tandem with measures to improve their accessibility. They grasped that their town centres were a major asset requiring comprehensive rather than piecemeal management. But this was the exception rather than the rule. Most local authorities made little attempt to integrate promotion of economic development with other planning and transportation measures because few regarded them as a political priority.

This lack of integration between emerging policy priorities and the planning of town centres was due to the government's permissive attitude to new development and investment regardless of location, which raised a question about the priority attached to town centres. Many central government policies only related to town centres tangentially because they happened to contain appreciable numbers of private sector firms or potentially significant areas of real estate with redevelopment potential. Town centres possessed little intrinsic significance and were not treated as distinct entities in policy terms. For much of the decade the precise implications of government policies for town centres remained unclear. Retail policy was a case in point. Although it gradually became apparent as the decade progressed that the government was taking a more relaxed line on retail development proposals in new out-of-centre locations, there was still much confusion over the detailed application of government advice. As late as 1988, a survey of the top 500 retail and service companies confirmed that government policy towards large outlying centres was unclear to four out of every five companies. Consequently, they experienced difficulty when planning their own investment programmes (Davies, 1989).

Local authorities added to the confusion with differing stances depending upon their geographical location. Those without a substantial retail presence were keen to adopt the less rigid line taken by central government to attract new investment and jobs. Those responsible for existing town centres adopted a more cautious attitude to retail development proposals and were more diligent in carrying out retail impact assessments. However, subsequent government advice that such exercises were unnecessary except when weighing major applications for planning permission led to fewer such studies. The latter authorities also pursued a variety of measures to maintain the competitiveness of existing town centres. Typically, these included restrictions on change of use from retail to financial services on ground floor level, encouraging use of upper floors in shopping streets and restrictions on: the number of hot food takeaways; sale of goods from petrol stations; sale of goods in non-food out-of-town outlets and the volume of floorspace developed in any one location (DoE, 1992). Planning authorities' earlier efforts to protect town centres by controlling the type of goods sold in out-of-centre stores were, however, ruled out by government advice counselling them not to interfere in commercial matters.

By the late 1980s, town centres' commercial dominance was being seriously challenged on two fronts. Not only were new out-of-town retail locations developing at an alarming rate. Changes in planning legislation exposed town centre office markets to increasing competition from outlying business parks and from premises converted to offices from other uses in the remainder of the built-up area. At the time, however, booming economic conditions, the emergence of new forms of speciality retailing, the refurbishment of shopping precincts and high levels of development activity, bred a widespread confidence and suppressed concerns about the shift of activity away from town centres. The prevailing optimism also obscured the fact that considerable sums of money needed to be spent on remedying past design faults.

Another significant aspect of the lack of coherence in policy-making towards town centres was the failure to integrate economic development and transport planning. The government's deregulation of public transport, its bias towards road rather than other public transport investment and rejection of integrated land and transportation planning, made it difficult for local authorities and Passenger Transport Executives to modernise transport infrastructure in town centres to allow them to cope with the additional traffic generated by economic development projects. Although the

London Docklands development is not strictly a city centre development, it is the supreme example of the folly of not properly co-ordinating land use and transportation infrastructure. Some local authorities did introduce more progressive transport policies in the 1980s, such as park-and-ride schemes, new light rail systems and more sophisticated and comprehensive traffic control policies. However, the majority adopted a more piecemeal approach to reducing traffic with limited results. Fragmentation of control of public transport and lack of expenditure upon urban transport infrastructure in the 1980s resulted in additional traffic congestion in central locations and increased the attractiveness of more spacious, less busy, out-of-town locations. Following the rejection of pedestrian–vehicular segregation in the 1970s, a distinctive approach to transport policy in town centres failed to emerge. Throughout the 1980s, government muddled through without a clear alternative perspective and local authorities struggled, with limited resources, to find new ways of managing escalating traffic levels.

The concentration of both central government and the various local authorities on physical regeneration and economic development ignored town centres' social significance. In some respects, retailers led the way because new schemes were built to higher design standards and incorporated a more diverse mix of retail and other uses. Closer attention was paid to customer needs by providing crèches, ramps for the disabled, and leisure facilities. However, this was not mirrored by improvements in the public realm. On the contrary, the level of maintenance of public open spaces, visitor facilities, pedestrianised areas and landscaping, declined in most town centres as a consequence of public expenditure cuts and competing priorities elsewhere. Authorities responsible for historic town centres were an exception to the trend, however, because they continued to invest in the quality of the public realm to sustain their attractiveness to tourists, and hence local investment and jobs.

In sum, although important new indigenous growth sectors were actively promoted during the 1980s, town centres existed in a policy vacuum for much of the decade. Only after the boom subsided and recession set in the early 1990s did central government and the majority of local authorities realise that aspatial policies had led to out-of-town investment dwarfing town centre development. When the recession began to bite, the realisation dawned that some town centres were suffering badly from an accelerated decentralisation of economic activity and increased personal mobility. If they were to survive and prosper in the face of competition from large out-of-town retail developments much more concerted support and management was required. Furthermore, as transport congestion and pollution worsened and environmental issues became more important in the early 1990s, common demand grew for traffic restraint measures and encouragement of more environmentally friendly modes. This new consensus led to another dramatic change in public policy.

## Town centre management and re-investment (post-1993)

Although the Conservative government's third term in office, after their election victory in 1990, appeared to promise more of the same, events soon took a different turn. While local government expenditure cuts continued and competitive bidding for supplementary urban funding supplanted distribution according to need, there was noticeably increasing private sector frustration at the lack of strategic planning of public infrastructure. This paralleled a growing disquiet in semi-rural areas at the explosion of peripheral development and worsening widespread traffic congestion. Market-led development and minimalist intervention were now demonstrably inappropriate.

Government also regarded town centres in a new light. Research commissioned by the government highlighted the fact that new out-of-town retail development was diverting significant amounts of trade from traditional town centres and that recessionary conditions and the growing dominance of large retailers were making matters worse. Retailing and other forms of out-of-town activity were also exacerbating traffic problems because most could only be reached by car. This was adding to the economic costs of congestion, disadvantaging non-car owners and potentially jeopardising the government's commitment to reducing $C0_2$ levels. Potentially this meant that targets set out in the government's Sustainable Development Strategy, as a result of commitments made at the Rio Earth Summit in 1992, were unrealisable. By contrast, it was thought that promoting reinvestment within existing town centres readily accessible to public transport and encouraging a wider mix of uses in such locations might prove a more environmentally sustainable course of action. Travel distance would be reduced and multi-purpose trips promoted. Pioneering attempts at partnerships of local authorities and business interests to adopt a more comprehensive approach to the management and maintenance of town centres in such places as Halifax, Nottingham, Harlow, Redbridge and Falkirk also caught the attention of the government. 'Town centre management' (TCM), as it became known, was seen as an effective riposte to the threat posed by better managed purpose-built out-of-town centres.

Revisions in planning guidance unveiled the new orthodoxy. The revised version of PPG 6 issued in July 1993 was significantly entitled 'Town centres and retail developments' (DoE, 1993). The introduction of specific retail policies concerning town centres stemmed from the realisation that their retail functions were pivotal to their viability and vitality and that a better balance had to be struck between retail development in town centre and out-of-town locations. PPG 6 acknowledged, however, that a greater diversity and mixture of uses needed to be encouraged to enhance town centres' appeal. The guidance note also commended the concept of TCM as a way of raising commitment and improving joint working between public and private sectors, harnessing resources and ensuring better coordination of physical improvements, promotion and other activities. Traffic management and promotion of public transport were advocated to reduce town centre vulnerability to traffic and car parking problems. Such sentiments were echoed in PPG 13, 'Planning and transport', which advocated the location of new development in areas where a choice of transport was available and traffic calming, car restraint and better integration of different forms of transport (DoE & DoT, 1994). The government's emphasis upon demand restraint and more balanced use of existing transport infrastructure stemmed from a belated recognition that even a dramatic expansion in roadspace would not accommodate the projected growth in traffic. The circulars both recognised the need to plan and actively manage town centres and marked the rehabilitation of integrated land use and transportation planning, approaches which would have been judged heretical during the previous decade.

In the mid 1990s, policy and practice at a local level has echoed the spirit of government guidance. This was hardly surprising since many local authorities were already practising what the government had begun to preach. Encouragement to local authorities to submit package bids for integrated transport measures, government financial support for conversion of shops into flats, and the opportunity to use discretionary funding such as City Challenge, stimulated much greater local authority involvement in town centres.

One of the most interesting recent innovations has been the rapid spread of TCM, which shows both the potential and the limitations of current policies towards town centres. The Association of Town Centre Management has defined TCM as 'the effective co-ordination of the private and public sectors, including local authority professionals, to create, in partnership, a successful town centre – building upon full consultation'. It is widely seen as an effective means of co-ordinating public resources, levering private sector investment, and securing community participation to reach an understanding of a town centre's weaknesses and strengths and implement a programme of physical improvements, marketing and promotional events. Individual initiatives vary in their scope and purpose, organisation and level of resources. Usually, they focus initially upon 'janitorial' matters such as management of public facilities, environmental services and policing. Over time, however, most TCM initiatives embrace other issues such as forward planning, promotion of physical improvements and marketing and promotional schemes. They can also move on to tackle wider issues such as improving cultural facilities and stimulating the evening economy. These topics involve a wide range of tasks including liaison with town centre users, representing their views to service organisations, dealing with security issues, information services and promotional activities, facilities for different types of users, researching retail trends, co-ordinating service providers and promoting customer care.

TCM has assumed a variety of organisational forms, ranging from the traditional local authority-led bodies and consultative groups to forums of key organisations or formal public–private partnership bodies. Recently the latter have become more popular because their balance of public and private organisations has proved an important way of involving commercial interests and overcoming their traditional hostility to local authorities. Their membership usually includes local authority departments, town centre employers, business organisations, residents and users, landowners, police and transportation bodies.

TCM initiatives have led to the appointment of town centre managers to spearhead improvements, build trust between partners and ensure collective ownership of the improvements and independence from vested interests. While there were only a handful of such managers in 1990, the majority of local authorities or partnership bodies now have a manager or intend to appoint one. Customarily, town centre managers have limited executive capacity or control of funds. In exceptional cases, managers have been granted discretion to manage a proscribed capital allocation by local authorities and other sponsoring organisations. The formation in 1991 of an Association of Town Centre Management to provide guidance on establishment of further initiatives and promote and exchange good practice, has further consolidated this new profession. Other organisations such as the Civic Trust, Boots, URBED and COMEDIA also offer practical advice on town centre regeneration.

Although TCM is currently the vogue, there is a lack of comprehensive research into its impact on town centre viability and vitality. Many initiatives are still in their infancy. The results of research have been inconclusive. A survey of 2,000 users in eight town centres, for example, revealed that there was no clear distinction between the level of improvement achieved by town centres with TCM initiatives and those without (Association of Town Centre Management, 1994). On the other hand, the study showed that those directly involved, including retail managers, believe the adoption of TCM had achieved positive results in most town centres. There is a broad consensus that local authorities and other partners have become more proactive and concerned about the state and appearance of town centres. The degree of joint working has also improved, multi-disciplinary approaches have been better orchestrated, more attention has been given to accelerating physical improvements and heeding customers' views. The study confirmed that a large proportion of users valued town centre managers. Town centres' participation in the best practice networks has resulted in more rapid and widespread promulgation of novel and successful approaches to problems such as graffiti, fly-posting and drunkenness (Shaw, 1994).

Nevertheless, it is clear that lack of resources and problems reconciling the differing philosophies and interests of the partners has limited the impact of TCM. Funding is the fundamental problem. Despite the government's view that property owners should pay for TCM as it is an investment in the future, most initiatives depend heavily upon public funds. Private sector contributions are usually modest. Retailers are the most common source of private funding. But many refuse to make voluntary contributions because they believe they are already paying the uniform business rate (UBR) and often a supplementary service charge in shopping precincts for the same services. In any case many local managers of chain stores have limited discretion to contribute funds because budgetary allocation functions are handled by head offices and their brief is to concentrate on generating turnover. Small retail businesses simply cannot afford to make substantial contributions because of the recession and increasingly tight margins. Absentee landlords, like financial institutions, have a detached attitude and seldom make contributions to TCM.

Local authorities provide the lion's share of public funding for TCM. But they too are constrained by continuing reductions in central government grant, capping of local council tax charges, restrictions on the use of capital receipts and the replacement of local business rate by the nationally set UBR. Given such restrictions and the removal from local control of the business rate, many local authorities have little stake in the commercial success of their town centres and are tempted to pay greater attention to meeting needs elsewhere. Also, the recession limited their scope to use section 106 agreements to secure wider social and environmental benefits from town centre development. A battery of central government financial controls limit the extent to which local authorities can participate in joint schemes with private developers. Buildings can no longer be obtained free of charge from developers in return for transferring development land because their value is set against the authority's usable capital receipts, effectively adding to debt charges. Acquisition of land is only possible if it is sold within two years of purchase, otherwise local authorities are not permitted to set acquisition costs against the ultimate capital receipt. Finally, since the introduction of the UBR, local authorities seeking additional revenue have paradoxically found it more profitable to sell land for housing rather than commercial development in order to reap community charge income (Gregory, 1991). A survey of 150 local authorities responsible for some of the top 400 town centres in the country confirmed that lack of resources is a real issue (Hillier Parker, 1994). Only about one in five planned to spend more than £1 million over the next three years on physical improvements while almost half indicated they were allocating less than £0.5 million. Provision of capital as well as design assistance by Kent County Council showed how seedcorn public finance can lever other public and private finance and stimulate the formation of partnerships in ten local town centres. But this remained an exceptional case.

Many TCM initiatives struggle to engender a true sense of collective ownership because of the differing approaches and interests of the partners. Private sector interests generally prefer strong leadership by a town centre manager and a concentration upon tangible projects. Local authority departments are more concerned with policy issues and adopt a more consultative, consensual style to secure community involvement. The time taken by some local authorities to overcome excessive departmentalism, lack of corporate vision, lack of public participation and excessive bureaucracy has often exacerbated tensions between the partners. Identifying areas of common concern and interest has involved substantial effort which has made backing for measures harder to secure. Many balances have had to be struck. While most TCM initiatives centre on the retailing environment, wider commercial, cultural and social activities should ideally be supported too. If TCM simply mimics the practices of out-of-town regional shopping centre managers, there is a danger that they will be playing against such locations on unfavourable terms rather than developing town centres' distinctive assets.

Other constraints limit the scope for action. Although the external retail environment can be improved, individual property owners or lessees cannot be compelled to carry out improvements to the interiors of their premises. Implementation of plans can be delayed by minority objections to planning applications, in contrast to out-of-town development where developers are usually able to operate more easily. In many cases, progress is checked by lack of appropriate financial and legal powers or overlapping responsibilities. Some commentators have argued, for example, for a clearer division of responsibility for car parking, strengthened flyposting regulations and the need for further government encouragement of recycling initiatives (Hillman, 1988). All these difficulties suggest that while TCM is a useful organisational and managerial tool there is a danger that it will raise expectations unduly yet lack the capacity to fulfil them. TCM is no short-term panacea. If it is to prove successful in remedying town centres' major structural and institutional problems, a sustained commitment from the relevant partners and substantial resources will be required.

Other initiatives in the 1990s similarly appear to possess significant potential but have not yet achieved a marked impact. More mixed use development schemes are currently being mooted in many major town centres, and also a healthy, if modest repopulation of town centres is beginning to take place. During the 1980s, repopulation was limited to gentrified parts of London and areas of converted warehousing in the capital and also in Bristol, Manchester and Liverpool. Such accommodation became fashionable with young professionals because of its proximity to central office areas and arts and cultural facilities and the growing aversion to increasingly lengthy commuting trips. More recently, however, a pioneering campaign to convert empty spaces above shops into homes, the 'Living over the Shop' (LOTS) initiative, has provided social housing for lower income groups. The innovative element of this scheme was the introduction of a two-stage leasing arrangement whereby the freeholder or retailer granted a housing association a commercial lease in order to carry out necessary refurbishment work. The association then offered occupants an assured shorthold tenancy of between six months and five years and subsequently managed the property. The guarantee of vacant possession at the end of the tenancy and also freedom from maintenance responsibilities won over reluctant property owners who had previously been concerned that granting residential tenancies would have a detrimental effect on their property's commercial value. Since 1991 the DoE, Housing Corporations and other public sources have contributed £40 million of funds to the LOTS initiative and, by 1994, over 2,000 residential units had been provided in various town centres (LOTS, 1994).

Such schemes have proved valuable in raising awareness of the advantages of repopulating town centres. They have offered affordable accommodation with ready access to the full range of town and city centre facilities, additional rental income for owners and better on-site security for retailers. Patronage of nearby local shops has risen and greater self-policing has reduced the risk of crime, especially at night time. However, LOTS and other similar schemes have not yet had widespread impact. Physical constraints including problems of inadequate access, lack of separate entrances from shops, the cost of bringing premises up to required fire safety standards and the physical condition and suitability of the property for habitation can make refurbishment costs excessively high. Owners' unrealistically high 'book' values also add to costs. This has made some housing associations wonder whether such schemes are worth the effort, especially since the property could revert to business use within a comparatively short space of time if the property market should revive. Progress has also been hampered by lack of funds for administration and failure to direct available moneys in sufficient amounts to parts of town centres where there is a demand for conversions. On the other hand, LOTS and similar schemes, have encouraged private developers to renovate cheaper property on the fringes of many town centres for residential uses where declining overall demand for space has made such lower value uses once again a long-term economic proposition. Over-provision of office space in central London and some other city centres has also prompted conversion into flats (Barlow and Gann, 1993).

Change in central government policy and local practice in the 1990s suggest a greater inclination to support existing town centres and evidence of more progressive thinking. While it is too soon to identify the overall implications of this change of heart, the question remains whether too little is being attempted too late. Decentralisation and continuing desertion of larger towns and cities in favour of smaller towns is a long-term phenomenon. The *laissez-faire* policies of the 1980s paved the way for a decisive shift in economic and social activity. Such popular preferences will not be reversed easily, if at all. Only when the dramatic surge in investment outside traditional centres came to an end with the recession of the 1990s did the government call a halt to out-of-town retail development. While PPG 6 and PPG 13 have reasserted the commercial importance of town centres and put the brake on large scale out-of-town retail development, it is as yet unclear whether the current focus upon environmental sustainability and minimising travel demand will necessarily favour development in existing rather than new outlying centres. Even if physical improvements in town centres boost retail turnover and enhance their distinctive appeal, in the longer term their attractiveness could again be undermined by growing car reliance as it was in the 1960s. At present, tele-shopping and telework appear to have greater potential to reduce travel demand than exhortations to motorists to switch to other forms of transport which remain unpopular. But that would not help town centres.

As with TCM, words and rhetoric need to be backed by new powers and resources. Currently, the tools for the job are lacking. Responsibility for public transport is fragmented amongst a multiplicity of bodies. Business rates are collected centrally rather than locally. Dedicated funding for special urban initiatives is dwindling rapidly with the demise of the Urban Programme and consolidation of other grant regimes. Despite the recent change in government thinking, increasingly strenuous efforts to regenerate town centres at the local level continue to be frustrated by the national government's lack of practical support for local TCM initiatives and the underpowered, fragmented, and half-hearted implementation of policy at national and local level. Furthermore, some aspects of the deregulatory philosophy of the 1980s have survived intact. The government's approach to public transport and its revised Use Classes Order and General Development Order continue to frustrate local authorities' attempts to steer office development and employment into town centres. The vitality of town centres also continues to be affected by issues on which the government has remained silent. These include, for example, the plight of the small retailer, the lack of dedicated resources for TCM and the continued neglect of fringe areas where there is most scope for diversification and redevelopment of obsolescent secondary commercial areas.

## Conclusion

The legacy of different phases of public policy towards town centres suggests that policies have reinforced, even accentuated, economic trends. During the boom periods of the 1960s and late 1980s, government policy acceded to development interests and gave them full reign. In the 1960s it cut swathes through traditional fabric and in the 1980s it accelerated the pace of out-of-town development and decentralisation. During the 1970s excessive deference to conservatism meant that important transportation and restructuring issues were ducked. Policies in the 1990s have resulted from recession and retrenchment. Whatever the relationship between cause and effect, the treatment of town centres has hardly been a success story in policy-making terms. Each policy phase has generated as many problems as it has solved, either through excessive zeal and insensitivity or inertia and neglect. The piecemeal handling of functions such as planning, transportation, arts and cultural activities, environmental maintenance, policing, on a departmental basis by both central and local tiers of government has always militated against much needed coherent, integrated management of town centres. And often the policies of different tiers of government have contradicted one another. While current government planning policies towards town centres appear fine in theory and have secured a degree of consensus, in practice the overall effect of central government's actions is much less satisfactory. Many town centres will count the costs of past errors of judgement for a long time to come.

## References

Association of Town Centre Management (1994) *The Effectiveness of Town Centre Management*, Healey and Baker and Donaldsons, ATCM, London.

Barlow, J. and Gann, D. (1993) *Offices into Flats*, Joseph Rowntree Foundation, York.

Civic Trust (1989) *Creating the Living Town Centre*, Conference Proceedings, 27 April, London

Davies, R.L. (1989) 'Planning policies for major retail development', in Civic Trust (1989).

Department of Environment (1980) 'Development control – policy and practice', Circular 22/80, HMSC, London.

Department of Environment (1985) 'Lifting the burden', White paper, Cmnd 9571, HMSO, London.

Department of Environment (1992) 'The effects of major out of town retail development', Building Design Partnership and Oxford Institute of Retail Management, HMSO, London.

Department of Environment (1993) 'Town centres and retail developments' Planning Policy Guidance Note No. 6 (revised), HMSO, London.

Department of Environment and Department of Transport (1994) 'Planning and transport', Planning Policy Guidance Note No. 13, HMSO, London.

Gregory, R. (1991) 'Boom or bust', *Municipal Journal*, 6 (2), pp. 35–7.

Hillier Parker (1994) 'Quality in the public realm in town and city centres', Hillier Parker/Civic Trust Regeneration Unit, London.

Hillman, J. (1988) *A New Look for London*, report for Royal Fine

Art Commission, HMSO, London.
HMSO (1963) *Traffic in Towns*, reports of the Working Group and Steering Group, HMSO, London.
Holliday, J. (1983) *City Centre Redevelopment*, Charles Knight, London.
Living over the Shop (1994) 'Living over the Shop', leaflet summarising achievements to date, LOTS, York.
Shaw, M. (ed.) (1994) 'Caring for our towns and cities', Boots the Chemist and Civic Trust Regeneration Unit, London.

# Chapter 8
# Improving town centres' survival prospects

## Introduction

Regenerating town centres is about far more than just reviving their commercial fortunes. While many were once a much liked and valued part of the urban scene, they have become increasingly boring, predictable, overcommercialised places devoid of local cultural significance. It is little wonder that many are half-heartedly tolerated as a necessary inconvenience by those who have no alternative but to use them and increasingly avoided by those able to travel to more convenient and accessible, less polluted retail locations out-of-town. Remarkably few are a joy to visit or work in any more. There is a sense that something precious has slipped through our fingers. Although life was much simpler before the 1960s, the experience of going to town even for the apparently mundane business of shopping was infinitely more varied and stimulating than it is today. Shopping in town was almost an everyday experience that could involve a chat with a neighbour on the bus, the opportunity to appreciate different local stores, purchase local produce and cut-to-order cheeses, and enjoy high standards of personal service and friendliness as well as the repartee between bargain-hunters and market traders. Such was the variety of window displays and street scenes, and so congenial the atmosphere in Liverpool just after the Second World War that many of its inhabitants used to travel into the centre on the overhead railway in the evening just to window-shop! Many of those traditional qualities are disappearing fast. Town centres must adapt to a very different set of circumstances or perish. Retailing and consumer behaviour have changed dramatically and the clock cannot be put back. To survive and prosper, town centres' governing interests will have to invent a new *raison d'être*.

This has to be seen as part of a subject of much broader significance. In recent years, concern has grown that British 'society' is beginning to disintegrate and that individual lifestyles are becoming more atomised, detached, limited and self-centred. The reinvigoration of public interaction in communal spaces may be one way of stimulating concern for the wider urban environment. The growth of communitarianism and discussions about urban quality of life point to a common desire for new solutions and value systems and a renewed sense of wanting to belong to a vibrant, well-adjusted community. At the same time, there are signs of social disengagement, such as the retreat into the home as a fortress against the outside world, the opting out of collective services and the flight from the cities. These run in tandem with feelings of political disengagement and a decline of accountable and accessible public institutions. This could be a fertile breeding ground for extremism and further social dislocation.

This final chapter seeks to contribute to the growing debate about what needs to be done about town centres. In the initial part it draws out the main principles from a growing body of good practice about how to regenerate town centres and presents additional ideas on each theme. But these will not prove sufficient to arrest their decline and they present a case for more radical reform. It does not aim to set out a definitive guide of innovative regeneration policies and practice because identikit approaches rarely serve any useful purpose.

## Principles of town centre regeneration

To begin to reverse town centres' decline, local bodies must agree and act upon a clear set of principles for regeneration. Too often in the past there has been a lack of consensus and inconsistency of approach. Town centres' attractiveness and appeal has been damaged by wild swings from excessive interventionism to neglect and by the way in which some interests have repeatedly dominated others. Concern at the dullness and lack of conviviality of many British town centres compared with many European towns and cities, has provoked considerable reflection. It is recognised that the deterioration in the quality of the public realm has been directly attributable to the past failure of developers, architects, politicians and planners to take into account the cultural aspects of urban living, residents' behavioural patterns and psychological needs. However, as Appendix 2 shows, a consensus has developed upon what are the necessary ingredients of attractive town centres. Experts of varying professional backgrounds now regard as all important the promotion of a wider mixture of land use and activities, greater attention to the overall environmental quality of public spaces, and safety conscious design, respect for local cultural features, quality of access arrangements, environmentally sustainable measures and good overall management.

Achieving change on the ground will be a matter of collective attitude and will and also responsible individual and institutional behaviour. Alternative thinking will only achieve so much, however, for much present behaviour bars progress. At present, the right to do as one pleases matters more than responsibility and restraint, financial gain more than community gain, corporate power and prestige more than community service, tax cuts more than public expenditure, private more than public space, and most fundamentally, the countryside more than the town. Yet it is in our towns and cities – in which four out of five British inhabitants live – that the result of such preferences is expressed in continuing tensions and feebleness of the collective imagination. Even if a change is worked in the attitude of key town centre interests full realisation of aims will not follow unless they are buttressed by a set of legal and institutional reforms. Each is discussed in turn.

*Balance*

The wider, positive and negative, effects of transactions between individuals, groups and institutions upon innocent third parties are most apparent in densely built-up urban areas such as town centres. It is imperative that governing interests of town centres maintain a delicate balance between economic, social and environmental goals if the long-term future of town centres is to be assured.

Any strategies for regeneration must therefore balance:

- *economic viability* – ensuring commercial prosperity by maintaining a critical mass of services and attractions and a high level of accessibility;
- *distinctiveness* – ensuring that increasingly external economic development and social processes do not destroy but rather enhance local culture;
- *sustainability* – ensuring that urban areas internalise rather

than export their problems to other areas or successive generations;

- *social cohesion* – ensuring that usage of resources and spaces observes principles of equity and social justice.

Too often in the past the first goal has been emphasised at the expense of the other three, and town centres have become culturally impoverished and the scene of environmental problems and crime. Town centres should not be treated as islands. Compatible strategies must be pursued in neighbouring inner urban areas to a much greater degree or the regeneration effort will be dissipated.

*Variety*

The development of a much wider range of uses and activities in town centres will be increasingly essential for two reasons. Retrenchment can be expected in both retail and office sectors, the past mainstays of most town centres. This will pose problems but should be regarded as an opportunity to develop alternative uses. Also, much greater attention will need to be given to the quality of life of office workers and residents and the attractiveness of the shopping experience. Part of the solution could lie in further promoting the repopulating of town centres. The LOTS initiative has shown that reintroducing a residential element has many practical advantages. Re-urbanisation will reduce travel demand, car shopping and car reliance. However, much greater attention could be devoted to supporting initiatives in cheaper fringe areas and incorporating other uses there. A combination of the reintroduction of residential elements, traffic calming, quality public transport, and additional central leisure facilities could create attractive new urban villages which would supplement town centre retail custom. Interesting mixed use schemes have already begun to materialise. In the Temple Bar cultural quarter of central Dublin, a consortia of developers and architects recently won an urban design competition and implemented an integrated architectural plan incorporating residential accommodation, revised pedestrian access arrangements, streetscape and open space proposals with improved traffic circulation arrangements. The scheme has enlivened the area and transformed the local quality of life. Another innovative scheme is the self-contained and self-sufficient mixed use development known as the Custard Factory project in Digbeth, near Birmingham city centre, which incorporates arts and leisure facilities, business space and residential accommodation.

Extensive repopulation will only occur, however, if quality of life is looked at in the round. At present the quality of health, educational and leisure facilities in many inner areas needs upgrading to encourage a wider range of social groupings, including families, to repopulate central areas. Comprehensive redevelopment of cheaper fringe areas of major town centres for such purposes coupled with improvements in transportation arrangements, could yield valuable returns, too.

*Flexibility and innovative thinking*

The traditional commercial dominance of town centres has in the past bred a sense of complacency and conservatism among local business interests which has contributed to their undoing. Town centres must adjust to new realities and circumstances. Lifestyles are becoming more flexible and unpredictable given shifting working patterns. Leisure time during the day is being squeezed by longer working hours. Yet many town centre shops retain standard opening hours when they could be experimenting with alternative times, like evening opening. Few local authorities are seeking to boost the evening economy which could attract people who no longer work in the centre during the day. Neither have town centre interests been very successful in reaching the wealthy and growing Third Age segment of the population. Many centres remain the preserve of the young, especially during evenings. Perhaps traditional shopping formats could be reintroduced for those with more conservative tastes. With one or two exceptions (e.g. The Exploring Living Memory Museum, Blackheath) attempt are rarely made to recall what it was like to shop in previous generations. Townspeople's reminiscences, virtual reality techniques and putting up plaques showing shopfronts or logos of former occupants could all be used to tempt people back into town. Many property interests are also failing to adjust to changing circumstances. Changing accommodation requirements and the extensiveness of the contract culture both mean that space is increasingly demanded on a flexible basis. In a buyers' market, long leases and automatic rent reviews will surely be supplanted by rental arrangements geared more to tenants' needs.

*Customer care*

Innovative counter-strategies are urgently needed to cope with threats to town centre retailing, like tele-shopping. If town centres are to retain or even regain custom, the customer will have to be accorded much greater care and consideration than in the past. Retailers are increasingly realising that town centre stores cannot compete on price alone. They may, however, be able to offset higher overheads by offering superior personal service and thereby generate customer loyalty. Other possibilities include a greater amount of home delivery to save customers from transporting heavier goods, eased restrictions upon motorists picking up goods and improved facilities for storing goods on buses. However, shoppers are not deterred just by poor customer service from poorly trained, often underpaid, staff. Unwelcoming arrival points, lack of provision for those with special needs, low standards of street maintenance and unsafe car parking, all combine to deter shoppers from going into town at all. Customers will have to be wooed and made to feel safe and welcome. This will involve frequent user surveys to establish likes and dislikes and views upon what improvements should be carried out. Greater attention will have to be given to making public spaces attractive places in which to relax, and to integrating local arts and cultural activities into the overall scene. Greater ingenuity could also be displayed in exploiting town centres' indigenous assets. Many interesting facades of shops are barely noticed sometimes because ground floor fascias are so garish and brightly lit that they distract attention from the more architecturally interesting upper storeys of buildings. If owners of shops and other High Street premises could be persuaded to subscribe to a comprehensive floodlighting scheme, this would not only highlight the architectural character of a town centre but also improve its general appeal.

*Accessibility*

Although town centres' commercial health depends heavily upon good car access, reducing our dependence on the car will be essential for good urban living conditions (Pharaoh, 1992). Town centres, of all urban locations, are the least able to accommodate the car. For this reason car usage must be reduced by ensuring that fiscal incentives and disincentives for the use of different modes reflect their respective economic, social and environmental costs in full. Experience in many Dutch and German towns suggests that favouring alternative modes to the car creates a virtuous circle by freeing road space for additional residential development, social uses and landscaping, and improving local quality of life and further enhancing the viability of those modes. This might begin to overcome public scepticism about whether there are realistic alternatives to the car. The economic as well as the environmental case for encouraging public transport, cycling and walking is also strong. Economic benefits include the job and expenditure spin-offs from additional vehicle production, savings from less congestion, savings in health expenditure associated with air pollution, savings to developers in the provision of car parking, the beneficial effect upon neighbouring property owners, and a better working environment for employees. Cost–benefit analysis of usage of the respective modes of transport and the distribution of benefits in urban areas might also enable a reworking of the method of financing public transport so that costs are borne by a much wider constituency of beneficiaries as is the case in France.

*Employment creation*

In the past, town centres have been important employment locations and meeting places. However, continued application of new technology in both the financial services sector and the retail sector will progressively erode both of these functions. Many banks and shops could soon be completely automated and personal contact will be minimal. Large numbers of operatives and clerks will become unemployed. In future, perhaps, many will wonder whether a trip into town is worth the effort when it will be possible to use virtual reality techniques to shop from home. This picture may be slightly exaggerated but it does raise questions about the future role of town centres and the social effects of continuing job losses, especially upon already hard-hit urban areas where the majority of the unskilled or semi-skilled live. Part of the answer lies in offering personal, specialised services as already outlined. Town centres could also prove a focus for the activities of a new community service to patrol locations like railway and bus stations and provide other support services such as databases detailing availability of products. This would provide much needed employment and help to reduce fear of crime, so encouraging additional visits.

*Local production*

A continual theme running throughout the book has been the disappearance of the locally-run business and increasing control of town centres by powerful externally-based retail and commercial interests whose products bear no relation to the locality in which they are sold. They induce a collective amnesia amongst the town's inhabitants about their town centre and undermine any sense of belonging and stifle and enfeeble local imagination. Such trends will be difficult to counteract. But some means must be found to stimulate local sources of production which will force the giant retail chains and leisure operators to cater more for local tastes and produce a more differentiated range of goods. Town centres must be seen as showcases for locally produced goods if their distinctiveness and special appeal is to be salvaged. Local authorities could do more by encouraging the use of spare shop units, public spaces and cultural facilities as a stage for celebrating and promoting local manufacturers and artistic talent as well as better known consumer products. They could also put together local product directories to encourage the substitution of externally produced goods by local products. The growing supply of ethnic products in towns and cities with a cosmopolitan population shows that shifts in consumption patterns can add to the variety of the retail scene. More people would purchase locally produced goods if they were made aware of the job creation benefits. Other means of stimulating consumption of local goods would be to offer discounts to locally based employees and inhabitants and to experiment with ways of linking town centre retailing and Local Exchange and Training System (LETS) schemes where individuals exchange personal goods and services rather than use money.

### *Local accountability and information*

The pattern of citizen objection to the progressive destruction of many town centres' traditional character is puzzling. Public protest repeatedly manifests itself only when the bricks and mortar are in place and it is already too late. And yet informed public opinion could be one of the most powerful means of changing individual and institutional behaviour. One positive move might be to provoke popular debate and participation in advance by portraying key civic proposals using virtual reality computing techniques in prominent high street locations. Computer networks, including high street workstations and home computers, could also fulfil a valuable public information role. An extensive range of town centre services and functions could be transmitted in this fashion. Better consumer information based on rigorous testing could be used to tell shoppers whether goods on display were environmentally benign. Consumer advice on nutritional guidance might stimulate demand for local produce and also prove a useful means of preventative health care. Such media could also be used for imaginative and sustained local campaigns to persuade people to part company with their cars when travelling into town. Better public information and civic education might even lead to direct civic action such as clean ups, monitoring of air and noise pollution and boycotting irresponsible retailers and other interests.

Public participation is also important to ensure that TCM initiatives do not become too dominated by retail interests. The pressure to achieve positive improvements on retailers' own doorsteps could lead to the neglect of other aspects of town centres such as their social functions and the fringe areas which are less commercially significant but arguably more important locations for re-introducing a wider range of uses into town centres.

## The need for reform

Prospects for putting these principles into practice are mixed. Growing alarm at the uncertain future facing many town centres has concentrated minds and stimulated more forward thinking. However, earlier analysis has shown that the resources presently devoted to TCM are only modest. The fragmented nature of town centre governance and the economic pressures on local businesses will militate against necessary improvements. If these difficulties are to be overcome reform will be necessary in three main areas.

### *Resources*

TCM has been able to achieve many things requiring only a modest outlay such as improved dialogue and co-ordination. But many infrastructural improvements cost considerable sums of money and progress has been hindered by shortage of funds, unsuitable funding mechanisms and a lack of local control over resources. Clearly, the imposition of a supplementary charge upon businesses for TCM has neither proved popular nor viable because of the prior existence of UBR and other service charges. Yet, in aggregate, the present levels of funding are widely acknowledged to be inadequate. Since local authorities are the principal contributors of funds and most businesses feel they are already contributing to the cost of environmental services via the rates, there is a powerful case for giving the former a stronger stake in their town centres and increasing their local accountability by returning the UBR to local control. Alternatively, central government could issue them with a block grant by top slicing the National Non-Domestic Rate. Central government could also help by easing capital controls upon local authorities to enable more receipts to be ploughed back into further town centre improvements, relaxing property disposal rules and providing more resources for land acquisition and treatment. Tax relief on company contributions to TCM and construction of retail and commercial premises might help increase presently modest private sector contributions (HC Environment Committee, 1994). A Town Centre Challenge programme funded by the Single Regeneration Budget has also been proposed (Royal Town Planning Institute (RTPI), 1994). While this might lever in additional private sector investment, it would be important to clarify the basis upon which money would be allocated. To avoid the twin threats of unnecessarily funding reasonably healthy town centres or propping up lame ducks, indicators both of need and potential would have to be developed to support the selection process. Some of the indicators of viability and vitality recently identified by URBED provide a useful starting point (DoE, 1994). These could be supplemented by public attitude surveys and environmental audits, information on retail floorspace and other specially commissioned retail surveys. Such information would prove useful to policy makers whether or not the bid was successful.

Section 106 agreements are sometimes put forward as ways of channelling additional resources into town centres. While these methods have considerable merit, there is a danger that local authorities could be bought off and unacceptable developments receive planning permission. Another recent development has been the offer from developers of out-of-town schemes to contribute to physical improvements in nearby town centres. The developers of phase 2 of the Merry Hill shopping centre have given an undertaking that they would fund improvements in nearby Dudley, if the scheme was given the go-ahead. While superficially attractive, this sort of move should be resisted because it is only sugaring the pill. Such developers have money available precisely because out-of-town retail outlets owe their success to the custom they have taken from nearby town centres.

*Institutional powers*

While it is imperative that town centre organisations respond rapidly to emerging threats and opportunities, their number and varying interests militate against this. There may be virtue in experimenting with different organisational models. One option might be to establish town centre directorates containing all the relevant professional skills to facilitate a more corporate approach to the delivery of local services and to provide a direct conduit for dedicated funds. Alternatively, a more temporary inter-disciplinary task force could be set up which would not entail the same degree of re-organisation. In the case of town centres requiring drastic measures, it would be useful if local authorities and other interests could apply to government for designation of some kind of special urban initiative. For example, the experiences of Urban Development Corporations and City Challenge Teams in central areas of Manchester, Nottingham and Liverpool suggest that a focused approach and streamlined decision making can achieve results over a short timescale. In each targeted area public investment has generated additional private sector involvement, a more corporate and co-ordinated approach by the local authorities and other public agencies. It has also resulted in additional residential and commercial development, as well as new arts and cultural attractions and environmental improvements. Another option would be to create a specialist unit within central government for resolving complex land ownership and assembly problems in town centres, similar to the Land Authority for Wales.

*Support for small businesses*

While the town centre versus out-of-town commercial and leisure development issue has received increasing attention in recent years, little has been done to address the plight of small, locally owned businesses. In today's world of powerful global corporations whose resources and influence dwarf national governments, the odds are heavily stacked against small traders and companies. However, there is evidence that public policy can make a difference. The variety of shops in central Paris, for example, is at least partly due to the legal protection afforded to family-run businesses which prevent their takeover by larger operators. In Britain, much of the damage has already been done by *laissez-faire* government policies, governing mergers and takeovers and excessive use of compulsory purchase powers in the 1960s. However, more could be done to redress the balance. Rates and other charges effectively discriminate against small businesses because small premises are more expensive to rent per square foot than larger properties. Property taxes and overheads should therefore be geared much more to the ability of the business to pay. Perhaps there are grounds too for local companies receiving some sort of loyalty premium or discount because they add distinctiveness to the local scene.

Property owners have also caused problems. Large 'blue chip' tenants can cope more easily than small businesses with costly overheads incurred by institutional leases, rack rentals, upward-only rent reviews, full repairing and insuring leases, and luxuriously fitted out buildings. While the market may ultimately force institutional interests to realise that most tenants want more flexible, short-term arrangements, the recent recession has shown that they often only adjust their policies when it is too late for the retailers. The government should monitor tenancy law much more closely and take steps to protect tenants' interests, as they have done in the housing sector. Another option may be to encourage experimentation with turnover rentals where the scale of payment is geared to users' size and profitability. Such rental agreements also encourage property interests to take a closer interest in local commercial affairs. They already operate successfully in the United States. Issuing energy ratings for particular buildings and changing tenancy laws to include responsible behaviour within the terms of the lease might also help minimise business overheads and ensure that landowners behave in an environmentally sustainable manner.

In the case of dilapidated retail areas ripe for redevelopment, it would be interesting to see local authorities experimenting more with quotas for locally owned businesses. Local authorities could enter into partnership with developers on the understanding that a certain proportion of units would be provided at minimal cost and to a basic specification to allow local businesses to benefit from redevelopment schemes. Many local authorities have co-funded mixed tenure residential development in inner areas on this basis. Local authorities could insist on the incorporation of other uses in such schemes as well. Adding to the local distinctiveness and variety of the retail experience in this way should also be in the interest of larger chains as it might lure additional custom.

## Conclusion

It is difficult not to view the future of town centres with trepidation given the scale of the challenges they face. There is growing uneasiness about how such concentrations of fixed capital will adapt in a global market-place where multinational firms' notions of territorial loyalty do not extend much beyond the maintenance of a profitable balance sheet. The current overvaluation of property in comparison with other factors of production re-emphasises this point. It is open to doubt whether town centres will successfully retain their appeal or become by-passed by increasingly fluid movements of international capital and a growing focus upon the home as a location of economic, not just social, activity.

Town centres should not, however, be allowed to decline for want of an effort to resuscitate them. The case for regenerating town centres remains a powerful one. Their abandonment would impoverish the urban scene and create 'edge cities' without a heart to them. The absence of a centre to urban life could also lead to disorientation and breed a sense of alienation and desolation. The prospect that British towns and cities could increasingly resemble their US counterparts continues to haunt us. But despite their problems, British town centres retain many positive virtues. Above all they are meeting places which continue to offer rich possibilities of social contact and diversion. They facilitate mass access by public transport. They remain important centres of executive decision making and information exchange. They are still sources of increasingly scarce and important employment for inner city residents. To sacrifice their livelihood and future for the sake of more artificial out-of-town business and retail environments which have a limited design life, or for the dubious privilege of being cooped up in 'hoffices' all day long, would be folly.

The future of town centres is now a subject of public conversation as well as professional and academic debate. After two decades of comparative neglect, the government has recognised their importance in revised planning guidance and has begun to address some of the main threats such as car reliance and out-of-town centres. It is now widely agreed that in the 1980s, projects, events and particular quarters of cities were emphasised at the expense of the strategic, comprehensive view of the city as an integrated entity (Healey *et al.*, 1992). Town centres can only properly be understood in that broader sense. Analysis in this book suggests that present policies are inching in the right direction. Further practical steps and legislative measures will, however, be necessary to increase their chances of securing a viable future.

## References


Blowers, A. (ed.) (1993) 'Planning for a sustainable environment', Report by Town and Country Planning Association, Earthscan, London.

Civic Trust (1993) *Liveable Towns and Cities*, Report for Campaign for Liveable Places by European Institute for Urban Affairs, Liverpool John Moores University, Civic Trust, London.

Bianchini, F. (1990) 'The crisis of urban public social life in Britain: origins of the problem and possible responses', *Planning Policy and Research*, 5 (3), p. 4.

Department of Environment (1993) 'Town centres and retail developments', Planning Policy Guidance Note No. 6 (revised), HMSO, London.

Department of Environment (1994) 'Vital and viable town centres: meeting the challenge', URBED *et al.*, HMSO, London.

Healey, P., Davoudi, S., O'Toole, M., Tavsanoglu, S. and Usher, D. (eds) (1992) *Rebuilding the City. Property-led Urban Regeneration*, E. & F.N. Spon, London.

House of Commons Environment Committee (1994) *Shopping Centres and their Future*, Report and Committee Proceedings, Vol. 1.

Montgomery, J. (1990) 'Cities and the art of public planning', *Planning Policy and Research*, 5 (3), p. 4.

Pharoah, T. (1992) *Less Traffic, Better Towns*, Friends of the Earth, London.

Punter, J.V. (1990) 'The ten commandments of architecture and good design', *The Planner*, 5 (10), pp. 10–14.

Royal Town Planning Institute (1994) 'Memorandum to the House of Commons Environment Committee on shopping centres and their future', RTPI, London.

# Appendix 1:
# Methodological problems in classifying centres and measuring their viability and vitality

Most existing classifications of town centres are based upon their retail ranking. Centres can be ranked in several ways according to growth in rents, yields, sales, retail floorspace, number of shops, number of multiples, catchment area, pedestrian flows, or a combination of these measures. Each has its strengths and limitations:

- *Retail and office rentals* are used by many estate development companies to compile town centres' comparative performance but they are inevitably partial because of their orientation towards larger centres, focus upon prime pitch, and reliance upon volume of transactions for their reliability which can be a problem in a recessionary climate.
- *Yields* – rental income as a percentage of capital value – are particularly useful to prospective property investors such as pension funds. But they can be influenced by differences in rents, town size and volume of recent development.
- *Sales* are a good reflection of custom but they do not reflect the diversity of shop type especially if a town is dominated by a few large retailers or conversely by a multitude of small but none the less appealing shops.
- *Floorspace statistics* may, if disaggregated by age and type, give some indication of changing status but possess the shortcoming of not immediately reflecting underoccupancy, falling sales and declining confidence.
- *Multiple shop numbers* are generally preferred to aggregate numbers of shops because they take into account the perceptions of national retailers of the buoyancy of different centres. Hillier Parker and the Oxford Institute for Retail Management have produced a fourfold classification of over 800 town cen-

tres comprising London, metropolitan, regional and district centres on the basis of type and number of multiples (Reynolds and Schiller, 1992). While this classification is also a useful guide to potential investors, it has the drawback of covering comparison retailing such as clothing and footwear but not convenience retailing such as food and newspapers and does not take sufficient account of speciality or leisure retailing.

- *Customer profiles*. Retailers pay significant regard to the purchasing patterns of potential catchment populations but because these profiles vary so much depending upon the type of good and shop concerned, it is difficult to derive a more general classification of centres solely on this basis.
- *Pedestrian flows* are more of an indicator of business than retail performance because some may be window shopping or visiting the centre for other reasons. Common approaches to measurement have yet to be widely agreed.

The most convincing attempt to date to capture the relative health and well being of different town centres concluded that potentially the most revealing indicators were pedestrian flows and retail yield (DoE, 1994). The former measure was considered a good measure of liveliness and vitality and an important portent of private sector investment. The latter, measured over a period and standardised using prevailing rent levels to allow for variation in size of centre best represented a town centre's present and future viability. URBED recognised, however, that no single indicator fully measures the health of a town centre. They recommended that these two core indicators be supplemented by other retail indicators. This would include demand for units, number of multiples, retail representation and type of usage and vacancy rates, and an ongoing 'health check' of a town centre's range of attractions, accessibility, amenity and organisational and financial resources to capture fully the diversity in quality of different centres and their current and potential prospects.

Despite this increasing sophistication, many problems hinder accurate assessment of town centres' vitality and viability. Lack of comprehensive data is a key problem. Turnover data is no longer available, for example, since the government ceased to carry out a Census of Distribution after 1971. Much available information is heavily biased towards retailing reflecting traditional understanding of town centres' primary role. User surveys, when they are carried out at all, tend to focus on the shopping experience, and even then have sometimes failed to reach a crucial segment of the market – those who for one reason or another no longer visit the centre but need to be wooed back. Many surveys also rely on professional perceptions of a town's quality rather than the views of users and potential users. For these reasons town centres' social functions remain much underanalysed.

## References

Department of Environment (1994) 'Vital and viable town centres: meeting the challenge', URBED *et al.*, HMSO, London.

Reynolds J. and Schiller R. (1992) 'A new classification of shopping centres in Great Britain', *Journal of Property Research*, 9 (2), pp. 122–43.

# Appendix 2: Ingredients for creating attractive town centres

| Ingredient | | Organisation |
|---|---|---|
| *Mixture of land uses* | | |
| • | diversification and mixture of uses | Civic Trust |
| • | diversity and choice of activities, ownership, access | Comedia |
| • | mix of uses, tenures, age of buildings | Urban designers |
| • | – attractions, a critical mass and diverse range of shops, services<br>– vitality, liveliness, pedestrian flows, viability, capacity to continue to attract investment, yields, demand for units, space in use | URBED *et al.* |
| *Housing* | | |
| • | promoting higher density development and repopulating of mono-functional areas wherever possible for a mixture of social classes, coupled with provision of necessary social and recreational facilities | Civic Trust |
| • | – more attractive places to live as well as work<br>– increased amount of affordable housing relative to total employment<br>– improved quality of housing, reduction of densities, more 'defensible' space | Environmental planners |

*Social functions*

| | |
|---|---|
| • promoting balanced social provision so that no particular group feels disenfranchised and excluded | Civic Trust |
| • social equity | Urban designers |
| • remedy shortages of open space | Environmental planners |

*Economy*

| | |
|---|---|
| • rethinking the town centre economy e.g. more flexible working hours, opening times; promoting the night time economy. | Civic Trust |
| • – economic vitality: number, range of small businesses<br>– lively evening economy | Comedia |
| • selective decentralisation of employment | Environmental planners |

*Transport and accessibility*

| | |
|---|---|
| • – giving priority to integrated and advanced public transport systems, cycling and pedestrian networks rather than private vehicles<br>– putting pedestrians before cars and thinking of thoroughfares as streets rather than traffic corridors<br>– considering permeability and legibility as well as accessibility: signage, lighting, etc. | Civic Trust |
| • access – economic: range of prices<br>– physical: mode of transport, group, disabled, etc.<br>– emotional: mental maps, sense of belonging<br>– legibility: signposting, information | Comedia |
| • – accessibility<br>– permeability<br>– legibility and visual linkage | Urban designers |

| | |
|---|---|
| • – increasing provision of more continuous, attractive cycling and pedestrian routes<br>– progressive reduction in road congestion and traffic delays<br>– reduced car parking with priority for essential users<br>– increasing pedestrian-only and pedestrian-priority areas | Environmental planners |
| • accessibility: ease of access by different mode, quality of linkages, provision for special needs | URBED *et al.* |
| *Amenities* | |
| • well designed, co-ordinated and positioned street furniture | Civic Trust |
| • environmental quality | Comedia |
| • amenity: distinct identity, attractive public spaces, streetscape, townscape | URBED *et al.* |
| *Crime* | |
| • safety conscious design | Civic Trust |
| • security, safety | Comedia |
| • secure environment | URBED *et al.* |
| *Arts and culture* | |
| • – celebration and promotion of arts and cultural attractions particularly those of indigenous origin<br>– using the town centre more as a stage, e.g. for civic events, street theatre, community activities, public art, design competitions | Civic Trust |
| • identity: tradition, symbolism | Comedia |
| *Heritage* | |
| • respect for local context, heritage and important features in inhabitants' mental maps | Civic Trust |

| | |
|---|---|
| • going with grain of local history, tradition | Comedia |
| • respect for place | Urban designers |
| *Sustainability* | |
| • observing notions of sustainability by promoting greening, recycling, energy efficiency and environmental accounting | Civic Trust |
| • – less dependence on long journeys to work<br>– greener environment, more natural features, e.g. trees and water<br>– greater self-sufficiency of local areas for daily servicing<br>– better energy-efficiency standards in all buildings, greater use of solar gain<br>– reduced consumption of fossil fuels, more use of combined heat and power schemes<br>– reduction of total waste and greater percentage recycled | Environmental planners |
| *New technology* | |
| • exploiting advances in technology and telecommunications in order to enhance urban liveability | Civic Trust |
| *Urban design and maintenance* | |
| • securing the highest standards of urban design, management and maintenance | Civic Trust |
| • sense of place, aesthetic quality: frontages, lighting | Comedia |
| • – visual appropriateness: respect for context, history<br>– visual delight: rich materials, decoration<br>– human scale: social mix, personalisation | Urban designers |

*Town centre management*

| | | |
|---|---|---|
| • | – promoting town centre management involving public sector, private sector and the public in a broadly based partnership mechanism<br>– learning from best practice in other British towns and abroad but avoiding mimicry by working out local solutions with local agencies and residents | Civic Trust |
| • | – public/private ownership<br>– accountability, participation in decision-making | Comedia |
| • | – relative cost<br>– consultation | Urban designers |
| • | – strategy formulation involving audit, local authority/business/user partnership, drawing upon principles of good practice from elsewhere e.g. welcoming gateways, appropriate parking, attractive public transport, quality street environments, public safety, safeguarding key attractions<br>– action: organisational capacity and financial resources to make things happen | URBED *et al.* |

*Sources*: Punter, 1990; Montgomery, 1991; Bianchini, 1991; DoE 1993; Civic Trust, 1993, Blowers, 1993.

# Bibliography


Abercrombie, P. and Forshaw, J.H, (1943) *County of London Plan*, London.

Aldous, T. (1992) 'Urban villages: a concept for creating mixed use urban developments on a sustainable scale', Urban Villages Group.

Alonso, W. (1964) *Location and Land Use*, 16, Cambridge, Massachussets.

Appleyard, D. (1981) *Liveable Streets*, University of California, Berkeley.

Association of County Councils (1994) *Towards a Sustainable Transport Policy*, 2nd edition, ACC, London.

Association of Town Centre Management (1994) *The Effectiveness of Town Centre Management*, Healey and Baker and Donaldsons, ATCM, London.

Baldock, H. (1989) 'Town centre management: its importance and nature', in Civic Trust (1989).

Barlow, J. and Gann, D. (1993) *Offices into Flats*, Joseph Rowntree Foundation, York.

Beer A.R. (1991) 'Urban design: the growing influence of environmental psychology', *Journal of Environmental Psychology*, 11, pp. 359-71.

Benwell, M. (1994) 'Can transport be a private matter?', *The Chartered Institute of Transport, Proceedings*, 3 (3) .

Berry, J. *et al.* (ed.) (1993) *Urban Regeneration, Property Investment and Development*, E. & F.N. Spon, London.

Bianchini, F. (1989) 'Cultural policy and urban social movements: the response of the "New Left" in Rome (1976–85) and London (1981–86)', in Bramham, P. *et al.* (eds) (1989).

Bianchini, F. (1990) 'The crisis of urban public social life in Britain: origins of the problem and possible responses', *Planning Policy and Research*, 5 (3), p. 4.

Biddulph, M. (1993) 'Design of the British city public realm: directing transition', Department of Civic Design, University of Liverpool.

Birmingham City Council (1992) 'Report of proceedings at the city centre planning conference – February 1992 – the future of your city centre', Department of Planning and Architecture, Birmingham City Council, Birmingham.

Blowers, A. (ed) (1993) 'Planning for a sustainable environment', Report by Town and Country Planning Association, Earthscan, London.

Boney, S. (1994) Speech to Belfast Chamber of Trade and Commerce, September, reported in *Planning Week*, 2 (39).

Bramham, P. *et al.* (eds) (1989) *Leisure and Urban Processes: Critical Studies of Leisure Policy in West European Cities*, London, Routledge.

Bromley, R.D.F. and Thomas, C.J. (eds) (1993) *Retail Change: Contemporary Issues*', UCL Press, London.

Buchanan, M. (1988) 'Urban transport and market forces in Britain', in Hass-Klau C. (ed) *New Life for City Centres. Planning, Transport and Conservation in British and German Cities*, Anglo-German Foundation, London.

Christaller, W. (1966) *Central Places in Southern Germany* (translation by C.W. Baskin), Prentice Hall, Englewood Cliffs, New Jersey.

Civic Trust (1989) *Creating the Living Town Centre*, Conference Proceedings, 27 April, London.

Civic Trust (1991) *Mortgage Express Civic Trust: Audit of the Environment*, Civic Trust, London.

Civic Trust (1993) *Liveable Towns and Cities*, Report for Campaign for Liveable Places by European Institute for Urban Affairs, Liverpool John Moores University, Civic Trust, London.

Clifford, S. and King A. (1993) 'Local distinctiveness: place, particularity and identity', Conference Essays, Common Ground, London.

Comedia (1991) *Out of Hours: a Study of Economic, Social and Cultural Life in Twelve Town Centres in the UK*, Gulbenkian Foundation, Comedia, Stroud.

Commission of the European Communities (1992) 'The impact of transport on the environment', Com (92) 46, Brussels.

Commission of the European Communities (1994) 'Towards a better liveable city', City Action RDT Programme background paper, CEC, Brussels.

Confederation of British Industry (1989) *Transport in London: the Capital at Risk*, CBI, London.

Corporate Intelligence (1994) *The Retail Rankings 1994*, CIR Publications, London.

Courtney Research and Property Market Analysis (1990) 'Survey of retailers in major new shopping centres opened in 1990', Courtney Research, London.

Cregan, M. (1990) 'Open spaces and quality of urban life', *Landscape Design*, 6, pp. 12–14.

Davidson, M. and Bell, C. (1994) 'Out of town or town centre', *Estates Gazette*, No. 9409, 5 March, pp. 170–1.

Davies, R.L. (1989) 'Planning policies for major retail development', in Civic Trust (1989).

Davies, R.L. and Champion, A.G. (eds) (1983) *The Future for the City Centre*, Institute of British Geographers Special Publication 14, Academic Press, London, pp. 41–59.

Dawson, J.A. (1994) *Review of Retailing Trends with Particular Reference to Scotland*, Scottish Office Central Research Unit, Edinburgh.

Debenham Tewson Research (1990) 'Business parks – out-of-town or out of touch?', Debenham Tewson and Chinnocks, London.

Department of Environment (1977) 'Large new stores', Development Control Policy Note No. 13, HMSO, London.

Department of Environment (1980) 'Development control – policy and practice', Circular 22/80, HMSO, London.

Department of Environment (1984) 'Memorandum on structure and local plans', Circular 22/84, HMSO, London.

Department of Environment (1985) 'Development and employment', Circular 14/85, HMSO, London.

Department of Environment (1985) 'Lifting the burden', White paper, Cmnd 9571, HMSO, London.

Department of Environment (1987) 'The Town and Country Planning (Use Classes) Order 1987', Statutory Instrument No. 764, HMSO, London.

Department of Environment (1988) Amendments to the Town and Country Planning General Development Order', HMSO, London.

Department of Environment (1988) 'Major retail development', Planning Policy Guidance Note No. 6, HMSO, London.

Department of Environment (1992) 'The effects of major out of town retail development', Building Design Partnership and Oxford Institute of Retail Management, HMSO, London.

Department of Environment (1992) 'Merry Hill Impact Study', Roger Tym & Partners, HMSO, London.

Department of Environment (1993) 'Town centres and retail developments', Planning Policy Guidance Note No. 6 (revised) , HMSO, London.

Department of Environment (1994) 'Vital and viable town centres: meeting the challenge', URBED *et al.*, HMSO, London.

Department of Environment and Department of Transport (1993) 'Reducing transport emissions through planning', ECOTEC/ Transportation Planning Associates, HMSO, London.

Department of Environment and Department of Transport (1994) 'Planning and transport', Planning Policy Guidance No. 13, HMSO, London.

Department of Transport (1989) 'Road traffic forecasts', DoT, London.

Department of Transport (1990) ' "Traffic quotes". Public perceptions of traffic regulation in urban areas', report of a research study, Dr P. Jones, Transport Studies Unit, University of Oxford for Traffic Advisory Unit.

Dickens, P. (1988) *One Nation? Social Change and the Politics of Locality*, Pluto Press, London.

Downs, R.M. (1970) 'The cognitive structure of an urban shopping centre', *Environment and Behaviour*, 2, pp. 13–39.

DTZ Debenham Thorpe (1993) 'Business parks: prospects for the 1990s', Special Report, DTZ Debenham Thorpe, London.

Edward Erdman Research (1991) 'Traffic free shopping', Erward Erdman, London.

English Overseas Property PLC (1994) *The City of Tomorrow: Decay or Resurgence*, EOP, London.

Engwicht, D. (1992) *Towards an Eco-city: Calming Traffic*, Envirobook, Sydney.

Gilmour, J. (1994) 'Can towns still be the central attraction?', *The*

*Urban Street Environment*, 5, pp. 10–17.

Girouard, M. (1990) *The English Town: a History of Urban Life*, Yale University Press, New Haven.

Goldrick, M.C. and Thompson, M.G. (1992) *Regional Shopping Centres: Out-of-town Versus In-town*, Avebury, Aldershot.

Goodwin, P.B. (1993) 'Impact of new information technologies on the development of mobility – TSU 737', Transport Studies Unit, Oxford University, Oxford.

Gregory, R. (1991) 'Boom or bust', *Municipal Journal* 6 (2), pp. 35–7.

Groat, L.N. (1986) 'Contextual compatibility: a study of meaning in the urban environment', unpublished paper presented to the Annual Meeting of the Association of American Geographers, Minneapolis.

Guy, C. (1994) *The Retail Development Process: Location, Property and Planning*, Routledge, London.

Gyford, J. (1991) 'Does place matter – locality and local democracy', Belgrave Paper No. 3, The Local Government Management Board, London.

Hallett, S. (1990) 'Drivers attitudes towards driving, cars and traffic', Transport Studies Unit, Oxford University, Oxford.

Harvey, D. (1989) *The Urban Experience*, Basil Blackwell, Oxford.

Hayward, R. and McGlynn, S. (eds) (1993) *Making Better Places: Urban Design Now*, Butterworth-Heinemann, Oxford.

Headicar, P. (1992) 'The environmental challenge: implications for land use and public transport', in Swallow, K. (ed).

Healey, P., Davoudi, S., O'Toole, M., Tavsanoglu, S. and Usher, D. (eds) (1992) *Rebuilding the City. Property-led Urban Regeneration*, E. & F.N. Spon, London.

Herring Baker Harris and Intermarket Research (1995) 'The Cheshire Retail Study', Commission from Cheshire Local Planning Authorities, Herring Baker Harris.

Hillier Parker (1994) 'Quality in the public realm in town and city centres', Hillier Parker/Civic Trust Regeneration Unit, London.

Hillman, J. (1988) *A New Look for London*, Report for Royal Fine Art Commission, HMSO, London.

Hillman, J.(1993) *Tele-lifestyles and the Flexicity: a European Study – the Impact of the Electronic Home*, OOPEC, Luxembourg.

Hillman, M. (1993) 'Cycling and the promotion of health', *Policy Studies*, 14 (2), pp. 49–59.

Hillman, M. (1993) *Children, Transport and the Quality of Life*, Policy Studies Institute, London.

HMSO (1963) *Traffic in Towns*, Reports of the Working Group and Steering Group, HMSO, London.

Holliday, J. (1983) *City Centre Redevelopment*, Charles Knight, London.

Holman, C. (1992) *Cleaner Buses: Ways of Reducing Pollution from Urban Buses*, Friends of the Earth, London.

House of Commons Environment Committee (1994) *Shopping Centres and their Future*, Report and Committeee Proceedings, Vol.1.

Howard, D.F. (1991a) 'Public transport: the options', *The Planner*, TCPSS Proceedings, 13 December.

Howard, D.F., Gentile, P. and Peterson, B.P. (1991b) 'Accessible cities for the twenty-first century', International Commission on Traffic and Urban Planning 49th International Congress, International Union of Public Transport, Brussels.

Howard, E.B. (1989) *Prospects for Out-of-town Retailing: the Metro Experience*, Longman, Harlow.

Hubbard, P. (1993) 'The value of conservation. A critical review of behaviour research', *Town Planning Review*, 64 (4).

Institute for Employment Research (1992) 'Review of the economy and employment', IER, Warwick.

Jones, P. (1989) 'The high street fights back', *Town and Country Planning*, 2, pp. 43–5

Jones, P. (1991) 'Public attidues to options for dealing with traffic congestion in urban areas – what the pollsters say', Institute of British Geographers Annual Conference, Sheffield, 2–5 January.

Jones Lang Wootton (1994) 'The decentralisation of offices from central London – an annual special survey', Jones Lang Wootton, London.

Kenworthy, J. and Newman, P. (1989) *Cities and Automobile Dependence*, Gower Technical, Aldershot.

Kenworthy, M. (1991) 'Town centre management', *Municipal Journal*, 6 (2), pp. 28–30.

Laconte, P. (1992) 'Transportation networks in urban Europe', *Ekistics*, 352/353, pp. 93–113.

Landry, C. and Worpole, K. (1991) 'Revitalising public life', *Landscape Design*, 4, pp. 16–18.

Lasch, C. (1995) *The Revolt of the Elites and the Betrayal of Democracy*, Norton Press, New York.

Law, C.M et al. (1988) *The Uncertain Future of the Urban Core*, Routledge, London.

Living over the Shop (1994) 'Living over the Shop', leaflet summarising achievements to date, LOTS, York.

Lofland, L.H. (1989) 'The morality of urban public life: the emergence and continuation of a debate', *Places*, Fall.

London Boroughs Association (1992) ' "Out of order!" The 1987 Use Classes Order: problems and proposals', LBA, London.

London Research Centre (1992) 'Paris London: a comparison of transport systems', joint study with l'Institut d'Amenagement et d'Urbanisme de la Région d'Île-de-France.

Luithlen, L. (1993) 'Capital accumulation and office development in Leicester 1976–1990', *Journal of Property Research*, 10. pp. 27–48.

Lynch, K. (1960) *The Image of the City*, MIT Press, Cambridge, Massachussets.

Lynch, K. (1984) *Good City Form*, MIT Press, Cambridge, Massachussets.

Mayo, J.M. (1988) 'Urban design as uneven development', *Environment and Behaviour*, 20 (5), pp. 633–63.

McGee, J. (1993) 'Strategic issues in retailing within Europe', Oxford Institute of Retail Management, Templeton College, Oxford.

McGlynn, S. (1993) 'Reviewing the rhetoric', in Hayward, R. and McGlynn, S. (eds) (1993).

McNamara, P. (1986) 'Statutory plans for city centres', *The Planner*, 6, pp. 43–5.

Maslow, A.H. (1970), *Motivation and Personality*, Harper and Row, New York.

Montgomery, J. (1990) 'Cities and the art of public planning', *Planning Policy and Research*, 5 (3), p. 4.

Morgan, J.M. (1991) 'Cycling in safety?', Transport and Road Research Laboratory, Crowthorne.

Nabarro, R. and Key, T. (1992) 'Current trends in commercial property investment and development: an overview', in Healey, P., Davoudi, S., O'Toole, M., Tavsanoglu S. and Usher D. (eds)

(1992).

National Housing and Town Planning Council (1992) 'Living over the Shop: report', NHTPC, London.

NEDO (1988) 'The future of the High Street', Distributive Trades Economic Development Committee, National Economic Development Office, HMSO, London.

Newby H. (1993) 'Shopping as leisure', in Bromley, R.D.F. and Thomas, C.J. (eds) (1993).

Oatley, N. (1991) 'Streamlining the system: implications of the B1 business class for planning, policy and practice', *Planning Practice and Research*, 6 (1).

Oc, T. (1991) 'Planning natural surveillance back into city centres', Town and Country Planning, 9, pp. 237–9.

Oxford Institute for Retail Management (1990) 'Who runs the High Street?', Research Paper, OXIRM, Templeton College, Oxford and Bernard Thorpe.

Pal, J. (1993) 'Change in the high street: quality and retail provision', *Town and Country Planning*, 6, pp. 148–53.

Parliamentary Office of Science and Technology (1994) 'Breathing in our cities: urban air pollution and respiratory health', Parliamentary Office of Science and Technology, London.

Petherick, A. and Fraser R. (1992) *Living over the Shop: a Handbook for Practioners*, University of York, York.

Pharoah, T. (1992) *Less Traffic, Better Towns*, Friends of the Earth, London.

PSI Research Team (1991) *Britain in 2010*, Policy Studies Institute, London.

Punter, J.V. (1990) 'The ten commandments of architecture and good design', *The Planner*, 5 (10), pp. 10–14.

Rannells, J. (1956) *The Core of the City*, Columbia University Press, New York.

Relph, R. (1976) *Place and Placelessness*, Pion, London.

Reynolds, J. and Howard, E. (1994) 'The UK regional shopping centre: the challenge for public policy', Oxford Institute of Retail Management, Templeton College, Oxford.

Reynolds, J. and Schiller, R. (1992) 'A new classification of shopping centres in Great Britain', *Journal of Property Research*, 9 (2), pp. 122–43.

Richardson, R. (1994) 'Finance floods out of the High Street', *Planning Week*, 2 (13), pp. 10–11.

Roberts, J. (1991) 'Saturday in the supermarket car park – a blip in history?', *Town and Country Planning*, 7/8, pp. 204–5.

Roberts, J. (1992) 'Transport – Doctor, Doctor', *Town and Country Planning*, 3, pp. 86–7.

Royal Commission on Transport and Environmental Pollution (1994) *Transport and the Environment*, 18th Report, Cm 2674, HMSO, London.

Royal Fine Art Commission (1994) *Lighten our Darkness: Successes, Failures, and Opportunities*, Royal Fine Art Commission, London.

Royal Town Planning Institute (1988) *Planning for Shopping into the Twenty-first Century*, Report of the Retail Planning Working Party, RTPI, London.

Royal Town Planning Institute (1994) 'Memorandum to the House of Commons Environment Committee on shopping centres and their future', RTPI, London

Russell, J. (1990) 'Traffic calming and town planning', *Town Planning Review*, 61 (2).

Salata, A. (1983) 'Offices today and tomorrow' Centre for Advanced Land Use Studies, College of Estate Management, Reading.

Sawyer, M. (1994) 'Driving the men wild', *Guardian*, 18 May.

Schiller, R. (1986) 'The coming of the third wave', *Estates Gazette*, 279 (6297), pp. 648–51.

Schiller, R. (1988) 'Office decentralisation, lessons from America', *Estates Gazette*, 4, pp. 20–2.

Schiller, R. and Reynolds, J. (1991) 'Shopping centres – ranking British centres', *Estates Gazette*, 9117 (5), pp. 60–1, 81.

Scott, I. and Parry, M. (1992) 'The makings of a star performer', *Estates Gazette*, 9224, pp. 25–6.

Shaw, M. (ed.) (1994) 'Caring for our towns and cities', Boots the Chemist and Civic Trust Regeneration Unit, London.

Sherlock, H. (1990) 'Cities are good for us', Transport 2000, London.

Simmie, J., Penn, A. and Sutcliffe, A. (1993) 'The death and life of town centres', Bartlett School of Planning, University College, London.

Society of Motor Manufacturers and Traders (1994) 'Survey of buses and coaches', cited in *Guardian*, 28 September.

Standing Advisory Committee on Trunk Road Assessment (1993)

'Trunk roads and the generation of traffic', HMSO, London.

Steer Davies Gleave (1992) 'Financing public transport: how does Britain compare?', Report to the Bow Group, the Centre for Local Economic Strategies, Eurotunnel, Railway Industries Association and Transport 2000.

Steer Davies Gleave (1994) 'Promoting rail investment', for Transport 2000, London.

Stoneham, P. (1994) 'Limited shelf life for town centre retailing', *The Urban Street Environment*, 7/8, pp. 10–17.

Swallow, K. (ed.) 'Passenger transport: putting it to work', CICC, Welwyn.

TEST (1988) *Quality Streets: How Traditional Centres Benefit from Traffic Calming*, TEST, London.

TEST (1989) *Trouble in Store: Retail Locational Policy in Britain and Germany*, TEST, London.

TEST (ed.) (1992) *Travel Sickness: the Need for a Sustainable Transport Policy for Britain*, Lawrence and Wishart, London.

Tolley, R. (ed.) (1990) *The Greening of Urban Transport*, Bellhaven Press, London.

Transport 2000 (1994) 'Myths and facts: transport trends and transport policies, Transport 2000, London.

Trench, S., Oc, T. and Tiesdell, S. (1992) 'Safer cities for women: perceived risks and planning measures', *Town Planning Review*, 63 (3).

Turok, I. (1992) 'Property led urban regeneration: panacea or placebo', *Environment and Planning – A*, 24 (3), pp. 361–79

UK Quality of Urban Air Review Group (1992) 'Urban air quality in the United Kingdom', First Report, HMSO, London.

Verdict Research (1993) *Verdict on Out-of-town Retailing*, London.

Vignali, C. and Jones, P. (1993) 'Factory outlet shopping centres', *Town and Country Planning*, 62 (9), p. 240.

Walmsley, D.J. (1988) *Urban Living: the Individual in the City*, Longman Scientific and Technical, Harlow.

Westlake, T. (1990) 'Electronic home shopping: when does it begin?', *International Journal of Retail and Distribution Management*, 18 (2), pp. 33–8.

Which (1990) 'Traffic in cities', *Which*, October.

Whitehand, J.W.R., (1983) 'Land-use structure, built-form and agents of change', in Davies, R.L. and Champion, A.G.

(1983).

Whitehand, J.W.R. (1992) *The Making of the Urban Landscape*, Basil Blackwell, Oxford.

Whitelegg, J. (1993) *Transport for a Sustainable Future: the Case for Europe*, Belhaven, London.

Whitmore, J. (1994) 'Business parks', *The Property Week*, 13 January, pp. 25–36.

Wilkinson, H.W. (1994) 'Superstores and the doughnut syndrome', *New Law Journal*, 28 January, pp. 136–7.

World Wildlife Fund (1990) 'Public attitudes towards transport and pollution', WWF, Godalming.

Worpole, K. (1992) *Towns for People*, Open University Press, Buckingham.

# Index